WOMEN

of the

WEST COAST

THEN *and* NOW

WOMEN
of the
WEST COAST

THEN *and* NOW

by
MARNIE ANDERSEN

Illustrated by
TAGE ANDERSEN

Sand Dollar Press

Poem "Dark Cloud: Fairest Day" reprinted by permission of
author. Poem "Meares Island" reprinted by permission of author.

Canadian Cataloguing in Publication Data
Andersen, Marnie, 1932–
  Women of the west coast—then and now

ISBN 0-9696986-0-7

1. Women—British Columbia—Pacific Coast—Biography.
2. Pacific Coast (B.C.)—Biography. 3. Pacific Coast (B.C.)—
History. I. Title.
FC3805.A53 1993   971.1'1'0099   C93-091278-0
F1086.8.A53 1993

Cover "Clayoquot Sound" and illustrations by Tage Andersen.
Printed and bound in Canada.

Sand Dollar Press
P.O. Box 2063
Sidney, B.C.
V8L 3S3

To
Women of the west coast —
wherever they may be.

Contents

Part One – Then

Part Two – Now

ACKNOWLEDGEMENTS

To Jocey Hanson, Mary MacLeod, and Dylis Bruce, my friends and generous landladies, west coasters all. I'll miss our "coffee and conversation sessions." To Maggie Kortes, who read the script with a practiced and caring eye. To Neil Stewart, who introduced me to the wonderful world of word processing, with enthusiasm and infinite patience. To my husband Tage, whose illustrations add depth and texture to the stories. And lastly, to my daughters, Karen, Elizabeth, and Dana, whose understanding of this project grew with time. Without the love of my family this book would not have been possible.

AUTHOR'S NOTES

For years we visited the west coast on holiday—enjoying the laid-back ambience of Vancouver, the scenic trip by ferry to Vancouver Island, and the Olde World gentility of Victoria. Then, by happy accident, we discovered the *west,* west coast and came to know and admire some west coasters, many of whom were women.

I began hearing stories, wonderful stories, about people born on, or transplanted to, the west coast. It seemed to me that someone should be writing them down. I started to hope, and later to plan, to somehow have a part in recording these stories. Next I set about collecting books on the west coast, and, as I read the stories, one thing became abundantly clear. While there were some wonderful tales about the coast and its people, particularly the pioneers, there was rarely any mention of the west coast woman.

Had she been imported—like Mandarin oranges—once the men had tidied up the land, built the homestead, and tilled the soil? Or had she, as I suspected, been there from the beginning, creating homes and raising children under conditions that were truly daunting?

After resigning from my mind-dulling job in Edmonton, and temporarily abandoning my family, I flew to Nanaimo. There I bought a respectably decrepit car, in a fitting rust colour. (I had no desire to stand out in a west coast crowd.)

Next, I set out over the mountains, heading west by north-west, until I reached the small fishing village of Tofino. I set up headquarters in a beautifully appointed cabin overlooking the inlet, and tried to convince myself that I was roughing it. Early the next morning, in the local ships' chandlery, I purchased a sou'wester, a pair of rubber boots, and a pen guaranteed to write underwater.

I'm sure, in more scholarly endeavours, researching the subject of a projected book can be tedious or even—dare I say it—downright boring. In this case, the research was downright exciting, challenging, and mind-broadening. Without exception, every west coaster I met, be they men or women, expressed great interest in the project and went out of their way to be of assistance.

They endured my many questions, no matter how foolish, overlooked my vast ignorance of matters marine, and never refused even my most outrageous requests. I talked with women in native villages and fishing boats, lighthouses and floathouses. I gained knowledge of such disparate subjects as: how to launch oneself from a bobbing Zodiac with a minimal loss of dignity and skin, the secret of the stars-in-the-water phenomenon, and the long range effects of mankind's environmental madness.

My older friends took me—in my imagination—back to the earlier, gentler, but no less challenging days of the settling of the west coast. When the biggest excitement of their lives was, depending upon their age (and marital status), the arrival of the *Princess Maquinna*—their only link with the outside world—or the weekly dance in the community hall. When an outing to the general store meant a six-hour hike (round trip) through dense rainforest, or a trip down the inside passage by rowboat.

Today the west coast woman often arrives by van. She is likely to be jolted by the west coast experience while paddling a kayak, hiking the Meares Island nature trails, or observing whales feeding in the wild. However it happens—to any one of us—the experience is unforgettable, and often requires a complete change in lifestyle. Some go home, pack up their belongings, and migrate west, others simply reassess their values and priorities, while still others sit down and write about it.

No matter the difference in age, background, or colour of skin, the women of the west coast are members of a unique sisterhood. Their respect for nature, capacity for hard work, and love of life, are just a few of their inherent attributes. The west coast woman experiences a delicious freedom, tempered by responsibility for herself, her family, and her planet.

Like many quiet corners of the world, the west coast is changing. No matter how we resist change, particularly in areas we consider to be inviolate, perhaps the best we can hope for is some measure of democratic control of the process. May we always recognize, and make allowances for, the seemingly diverse needs of man and nature. May we realize that, in the end, they are the same.

INTRODUCTION

For those readers who may be unfamiliar with Canada's *west,* west coast, some orientation might be helpful in order to appreciate its vibrant history and exciting and ever controversial future. Vancouver Island, named for the British sea captain who surveyed the island from 1792–1794 is the undisputed jewel of the Pacific Northwest. Washed by the Japanese current (Kuroswio) and swept by the western trade winds, it offers a salubrious climate, heart-stirring vistas, and tranquility for the soul. Situated on the island's southernmost shores, Victoria is the capital city of British Columbia.

Before the turn of the century, long before it became overlaid with a fragile patina of European elegance, Victoria was a sprawling, brawling, frontier settlement. Its polyglot population ranged from Chinese labourers to black American entrepreneurs, from Hawaiian sailors to Greek fishermen. At the same time, Indian tribes within the area were slowly being displaced to the perimeters of the land to which the newcomers arrogantly laid claim. Victoria had the largest red-light district in the Pacific Northwest and an active opium industry which was not legally closed down until 1907. The entire Vancouver Island was leased to the Hudson's Bay Company for a nominal yearly fee.

In the early part of the twentieth century, Vancouver Island experienced a boom, due in part to American investment in the island's timber and mining resources. Europeans were drawn to Canada's west coast by the promise of free land and an opportunity to reshape their fortunes in the new world, unhindered by feudal class systems. Within a few years, the immigrants, predominantly English, had transformed this raw Canadian town, named for their queen, into a genteel replica of England. It was complete, some said, with a more modern type of class system.

Far from the cream teas and garden parties of Victoria lay the rugged west coast of the island. A region of savage beauty, it attracted adventurers and artists, prospectors and missionaries, traders and n'er-do-wells. It held a promise of opportunity for those willing to forsake the comforts of the cities, for those with a dream. This was the area whose waters became known as the "Graveyard of the Pacific," in reference to the more than four hundred vessels which met with disaster on the reefs. Commercial fishing and logging were opening up the area and gold had been discovered in the rugged mountains. A prosperous future was forecast for the island's newest frontier. In 1912, when Long Beach was first settled, the C.P.R. planned to build a rail line out to the island's west coast, but war broke out in Europe and the idea was never revived.

As a consequence, most newcomers arrived by Canadian Pacific steamship, although a good number of hardy souls took the coach line from Victoria to Port Alberni and from there hiked in over the telegraph trail that ran over, around, and through the MacKenzie mountain range. Once on the other side, the trail ran alongside Kennedy Lake, largest body of fresh water on the island, and, in early times, site of a flourishing fish cannery and a logging camp. Further on, the trail split, with one arm turning south to the bustling deep sea port of Ucluelet, an Indian name meaning "safe harbour."

The other arm of the trail ran north, bisecting the Esowista peninsula. It opened onto the breathtaking panorama of a twelve-mile crescent of white sandy beach, sculptured by foam-topped breakers, and backgrounded by coastal mountains. It appeared on nautical charts as Wickaninnish Bay (although local people always knew it as Long Beach, or simply "the beach"), named for the Indian chief who ruled over the Clayoquot tribe and who maintained a summer residence on its shores. From here the trail continued north, to end in the tiny fishing village of Tofino, named for a Spanish hydrographer.

And here, on the outer coast of Vancouver Island, is where the romance begins. Much of it is reflected in the colourful names that dot the area, names that can only hint at the influence of the First Nations, the Spanish and the English and later the settlers, from all points of the globe.

The west coast woman was always there, from the first Indian princess to the sea captain's wife, from the settler's mail-order bride to the lighthouse keeper's mate. All helped make the west coast what it is today.

The "West" West Coast

Labels on map:
TATUS
NOOTKA
NOOTKA SOUND
ESTEVAN POINT
BOAT BASIN
CLAYOQUOT SOUND
TOFINO
WICKANINNISH BEACH
UCLUELET
BARKLEY SOUND
BAMFIELD
MACKENZIE RANGE
STRATHCONA PARK
SPROAT STREAM
VANCOUVER ISLAND
BEAUFORT RANGE
PORT ALBERNI
COURTENAY
PARKSVILLE

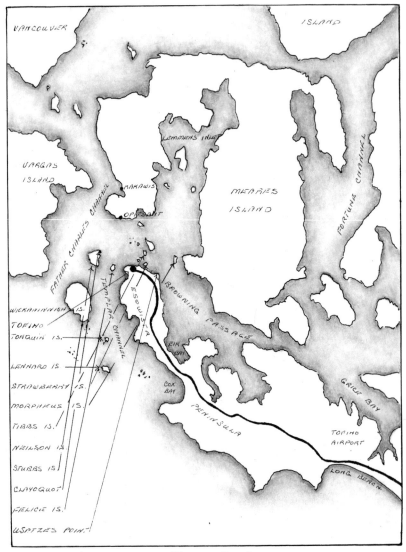

Clayoquot Sound

Part One
THEN

ONE

Cougar Annie

In the year 1915, at the age of twenty-seven, Annie and her husband Willie, together with their three small children, turned their backs on civilization as they knew it, and sailed from Vancouver aboard the schooner *Tees* to the wild north-west coast of Vancouver Island. They eventually settled at Boat Basin in Hesquiat Harbour. Annie would bear five more children in the wilderness, claw a living out of the harsh, unforgiving environment practically singlehandedly—despite the addition over the years of three mail-order husbands—and in the process become a west coast legend. She was a tiny woman, blessed with surprisingly strong, capable hands, hands that were equally at ease tending her babies, clearing brush, or wielding a twenty-gauge shotgun in her role as registered bounty hunter.

Annie was born in California in 1888 and shortly thereafter the family moved to South Africa where her father George was active in the Boer War as a commander in the Royal Engineers. The pretty young girl—she had long glossy black hair, which her mother kept in ringlets, sparkling eyes, and a charming manner—was schooled in Johannesburg and England, and graduated with honors. At the age of fifteen she attended business college, later received her teacher's certificate, and found employment with the Monastery Diamond Mines in Johannesburg. When the war ended, the family emigrated to Canada.

George purchased a farm in northern Alberta with monies received from the army upon his retirement. The family considered Annie's mother Margaret too much of a lady to help with the menial farm chores, and so Annie, an only child, found herself working alongside her father, doing everything from herding cattle to chopping wood. George also taught his daughter how to handle a rifle, a skill that would prove valuable in the years to come. The first year the crop failed, and, after the second summer, when an uncontrollable prairie fire destroyed the farm, they moved to Winnipeg.

George got his family settled and then left for several years to study veterinary medicine at a college in Illinois. Annie worked during this time as a stenographer in the large mail-order department at Eatons department store. She was efficient and well liked, and when an opening for office manager became available, Annie was awarded the position at the tender age of nineteen. Later, when George obtained his degree, he returned to Canada, set up his practice in Vancouver, and sent for Margaret and Annie. With some reluctance, Annie resigned her position and the two women travelled west on the newly-laid Canadian railway.

Once again Annie quickly found a good clerical position, this time with the Bank of Hamilton. In her spare time she worked in her father's clinic, and it was here that she met Willie, a young Scotsman, when he brought in his ailing terrier. At that time Willie was working as an orderly in a Vancouver hospital. He had exhausted the considerable inheritance bequeathed to him by his aristocratic father, former Lord Mayor of Glasgow. In later years it was discovered that Willie had been banished from Scotland and held on the Isle of Man for five years. The exact nature of the crime was never revealed.

The two became friends, and later Annie, at the urging of her parents, who considered Willie a great catch, agreed to give up her job at the bank and marry him. The young couple became partners in the animal clinic and, in addition, Annie ran a profitable business in the buying and selling of dogs. For fifteen dollars a month they rented a large house situated on four acres of land on Granville Street. It was in this house that their first three children were born.

The early years of the marriage were, by all accounts, happy ones for Annie. She found a sense of fulfillment in her marriage and motherhood as well as her work in the clinic. She had every reason to expect her life to continue along this comfortable, if somewhat unremarkable path for years to come. However, fate had other plans for Annie.

Willie had begun to drink heavily, and was also known to frequent the opium dens of Chinatown. As a result, he began to neglect his family and frequently missed work. As their debts increased, Annie grew worried and finally confronted Willie. In a desperate attempt to save his health, and also salvage their marriage, the couple pulled up stakes. They sailed with their three toddlers for the west coast of Vancouver Island where they preempted 117 acres of prime land in one of the most isolated and stunningly beautiful areas in British Columbia. Although there is no record of George ever seeing his beloved daughter again, they remained close, exchanging warm and loving letters through the years. He also managed, occasionally, to send funds.

The small family, hastily transplanted from the city, found themselves at first almost overwhelmed by the wilderness. Their only neighbours in those early years were natives of the Hesquiat tribe, whose village was nearby. A small, ramshackle building stood on the property, and it was in this rough-hewn one-room cabin that Annie, over the next few years, gave birth to five more babies—with no one to assist her but Willie.

Several years later, when the original cabin burned to the ground, a new one was built at a location set back from the beach and protected by trees. It consisted of three bedrooms, a kitchen, and a roomy attic. In later years a water line was laid from the house to a small lake nearby. Unfortunately, the bears of the area were fascinated by the sound of the water running through the pipe and continually dug it up.

As fate would have it, Willie proved to be entirely unsuited to life in the wilderness, consequently the bulk of the outside work fell to Annie. Rising at first light, before the family stirred, she was out on the land—burning and clearing and planting—often working until well after dark. In a division of labour years ahead of its time, Willie preferred to stay inside and look after the children.

Many times in those early years, before fully establishing themselves, the young family hovered on the brink of starvation. The story is told that Annie, after having her vegetable garden ravaged by storms, set out with her rifle one cold fall day in search of one of the wild cows that roamed the area, remnants of early settlers' herds. She became confused, and finally lost, in the dense rain forest and was forced to spend the night in a cave. Also seeking refuge in the dark and gloomy cavern was a family of raccoons. Annie was too exhausted to care, and fell asleep with her hand on her rifle. Late the following day, local natives found her, by now ill with fever and delirium, and carried her to their village where they nursed her back to health.

Throughout the years, Annie maintained good relations with the native people of the area. She was often called upon to act as mid-wife at a difficult delivery, being paid with gifts such as fish or trading beads. She continued to clear the boggy land, hacking out trails and building drainage ditches and boardwalks between the garden areas where necessary. As well, various storage sheds and chicken coops began to appear, until the property began to resemble a miniature frontier village. She decided to raise goats, chickens, and rabbits to supplement the vegetables she grew, and later ran a trap line around Hesquiat Lake. She was successful in catching marten and mink, whose skins she sold to the Hudson's Bay Company.

Willie soon came to think of himself as a gentleman farmer and spent much of his time, when not involved with the children, fashioning small chicken coops and bird houses, some of which were rather extravagantly embellished with curlicews and gingerbread trim. He also enjoyed sitting for hours writing poetry and reading. A missionary who visited the family during these years was shocked to discover Willie using pages of the family Bible in which to roll his cigarettes!

The children worked alongside their mother from an early age. Their chores included tending the goats, which eventually numbered over one hundred, finding feed for the rabbits (who multiplied at a healthy rate), gathering driftwood from the beach for the fire, and hauling water from the creek that ran through the property. The chickens were allowed to run free during the day and, as a result, the finding and gathering of their eggs was a never-ending chore. Once a month it was the duty of the two older children to row out into the bay in a dug-out canoe (often late at night) to meet the supply ship *Princess Maquinna*. Many times they were forced to wait several hours as the time of arrival was, of necessity, approximate. The children would off-load supplies and mail and deliver them to the house. It was a harsh life: there were always more chores than there were hands to do them. Consequently, when the children grew older, most left and never returned.

On a bright summer day in 1936, after twenty-one years at Boat Basin, Willie drowned in the bay. Early that morning he paddled out in his little wooden boat to do some fishing, and, as the day warmed, stood to remove his jacket. He lost his balance and fell overboard with his arms still in the sleeves. No one heard his frantic cries for help. Annie conducted a simple service and buried him in the garden.

Unable to manage alone, the former mail-order clerk placed an ad in the *Winnipeg Free Press* for a gentleman to come west for employment on the farm. Several weeks later he arrived by mission boat and they were married the same evening. Unfortunately this marriage was short lived as he shot himself while cleaning his gun and bled to death. Once again Annie advertised for a husband and they were married for several years before he succumbed to pneumonia. Many years later she placed another ad and married one final time, only to be forced to run that man (no gentleman) off the place after he attempted to kill her in order to inherit the homestead!

As Annie gradually tamed the land, she conceived the idea of raising bulbs, berries, and fruit trees to supplement her income. Ultimately she had a small orchard which produced pears, apples, plums, cherries and raspberries. She experimented, grafting domestic apples to wild, and the hybrid fruit produced was pronounced by visitors as some of the best they'd ever tasted. Much of the produce grown on the farm had never before been grown on the west coast. She opened a tiny store in her home where she stocked a few staples and sold fruits, vegetables, and fresh eggs to the natives and few fishermen of the area. Annie took great pride in her eggs, sending most of them south to be sold in the Co-Op store in Tofino. She also grew dahlias, rhododendrons, and azaleas, a delight to the eye for weary travellers in that most unlikely location.

However, it was her mail-order dahlia bulb business that gave Annie the most satisfaction. She began by advertising the bulbs in papers across Canada, and the enterprise grew to the point where she contracted to operate a small post office, also within her home. Before long, orders began arriving from all over the world, addressed to:

Post Mistress
Boat Basin Post Office
British Columbia
Canada

Annie packed her bulbs carefully, wrapping them in dried ferns, chicken feathers, or moss and always including a few extra. Her customers often wrote her appreciative letters, sometimes including pictures of their families. In this way the lonely woman in the wilderness once again established contact with the outside world. Eventually a large storeroom was added to the house. It contained dozens of neatly stacked boxes in which hundreds of bulbs lay in rows between layers of newspaper. Each box was carefully labelled as to which type and colour they contained. Late at night, when the house was quiet, she would sit and type up her orders on an ancient little typewriter by the light of a coal oil lamp. They were sent out by way of the *Maquinna* or the mission boat which visited regularly. She maintained her business until well into her eighties, when some far removed mandarin in the postal service learned her age and cancelled the contract for Boat Basin.

Marauders were always a problem on the farm. Bears and deer enjoyed eating the fruit and bulbs, mink and raccoons appreciated the eggs, and wolves always lurked nearby. In an attempt to keep losses to a minimum, wire fences were built around the garden plots and traps were laid for the small animals. Consequently, wandering around the property at night could be very dangerous.

By far the most serious problem, however, was the presence of cougars. During the 1920s a mysterious liver disease killed many of the deer on the west coast and, as a result, cougars increased their attacks on farm animals. Annie was forced to protect her family and animals and always kept a loaded rifle nearby. Numbers vary, but the plucky little woman—who by that time was a registered bounty hunter—is credited with dispatching at

Home – Boat Basin 1926

least fifty wolves, eighty bears, and seventy-one cougars. Visitors to the farm recall seeing large jars of cougar meat sitting in neat rows on shelves in her pantry. Thus, over the years, her nickname, "Cougar Annie," evolved. She never liked the title, perhaps not realizing that west coasters generally used it as a term of respect and admiration.

Annie's role as bounty hunter for the area took a bizarre twist involving her youngest son Laurie. A fisherman by trade, he stopped one day at the Indian village nearby to pay a visit to the daughter of the chief. Unfortunately for Laurie, a young man of the village (perhaps favouring the young woman himself), took exception to the visit. As a practical joke, he quietly removed the drain plug from the fishing boat. Laurie went down with his boat halfway between Hesquiat and Boat Basin.

Strangely enough, some weeks later, the jealous young native was attacked and eaten by a cougar. Annie was asked to track the large cat. After shooting the animal, she began to cut it up, only to find the remains of the young man's clothing in the cougar's stomach!

Of all the animals on the farm, the chickens were Annie's particular favourites and many had names. On the back of her large woodburning stove, she kept a cast iron pot of chicken mash simmering constantly. Into this she emptied all scraps and other odds and ends such as dead mice and birds. She often trapped blue jays as they were destructive. She would skin them and eat the meat before adding the remnants to the pot. She said she found them very tasty. It might be assumed that no one who knew Annie ever lifted the lid of that particular pot to enquire what was for dinner!

As the years wore on, Annie's life continued in rhythm with the seasons. Visitors to the farm rarely found her in the house. She was usually working in some far corner of the property, perhaps repairing a fence or picking fruit, even though in later years she was plagued with arthritis and her sight was beginning to fail. She enjoyed company but rarely did she have time to stop and visit. Instead, they were welcome to work along with her and at the end of their labours share a cup of tea and a thick slice of bread, spread with butter and home-made preserves.

Her only company during the latter years of her life was her youngest son Tom, who lived in a small cabin on the farm. He had worked on a lighthouse tender (supply ship) for several years before being badly injured in a fall into the hold. Thereafter he lived at Boat Basin and helped his mother. As one of her last actions, Annie set up a trust fund for Tom which would enable him to be suitably cared for during the remainder of his life.

Her oldest son Frank, a commercial fisherman, also remained close to his mother until his death and visited her often. His son David remembers visiting his grandmother on the occasion of his eighth birthday and being gifted with a baby goat. Annie usually wore a brightly coloured housedress, the neck closed with a safety pin, and her feet shod in gumboots. Her white hair was always neatly arranged on top of her head.

People remember her penetrating eyes of vivid blue— "the eyes of a seer" some have said. Most knew her to be shy and kindly, a lady in spite of her surroundings. She never tolerated swearing in her presence. When boaters would visit and ask her to pose for pictures she politely complied, quietly insisting that her left side was her best. In one of the photos taken several years before her death, Annie might have been taken for an English gentlewoman spending an indolent afternoon in her garden.

Eventually the surrounding area was opened up to logging and the feisty little woman quickly became a favorite with the men, most of whom called her granny. They all kept a watchful eye on the farm and its occupants. The first shift out in the morning always checked to make sure there was smoke curling from the chimney of the house. Often a truck would stop and drop a log off in front of the gate, and soon another would come by and its crew would cut it into firewood and stack it outside her door. They sometimes brought gifts from the cookhouse, ice cream being a special treat to a household that never knew refrigeration.

Annie was presented with a wall crank telephone, one of the first on the coast, and it became a valuable link with the outside world. In later years, when it was to be replaced with a more modern variety, she requested that this be installed inside her original wall phone. One day, in her eighty-fifth year, she fell on a loose step and broke her knee cap. Although in great pain, she managed to crawl into the shed for a hammer and nails to repair the errant step before someone else was injured. That done, she dragged herself to the house, cleaned herself up, and then called for help. The loggers responded and early the next morning she was airlifted south to the hospital in Tofino.

As her sight worsened, Joe, the lighthouse keeper at Estevan Point, began to visit once a month and the two became warm friends. Joe would sit at her desk doing the accounts while Annie sat close by pruning her beloved dahlia bulbs. Once finished, they would share a simple meal. Joe remembers that, while there were several clocks in the house, none of them ever ran—as though the passing of time were no longer a concern in Annie's life. The mission boat was always welcomed and often a simple service was held in her home.

In the twilight of her life, Annie lost her sight completely. Her memory was also fading and because of this the family became concerned for her safety. Upon consultation, it was reluctantly decided to remove her from the farm and transport her to a nursing home in Port Alberni. Thus, at the age of ninety-five, the gallant little woman left Boat Basin for the last time. Annie died at the age of ninety-seven.

Annie never considered herself a heroine, nor what she had accomplished in life to be extraordinary. She simply did what she had to do and scoffed at any attempts to enlarge upon it.

More than once in her later years, upon looking back, she said that she had enjoyed her life, hard as it might have been, nor would she change it if she had the chance to do it over again.

Today the weathered house and outer buildings stand much as they did in Annie's lifetime. The clutter and bustle have gone, however, and the place looks deserted. Because of the disappearance of the surrounding forest, cougars and wolves no longer frequent the area and bears are rarely seen. There is however, a presence. Those who stand motionless, who become one with the sighing wind and the sound of the surf, are not alone.

TWO

Ladies of Clayoquot

Clayoquot, the tiny frontier settlement where it all began at this end of the world, lies somnolent today, the lodge deserted, the former store leaning at a drunken angle as it slowly submits to the persistent waters lapping at its foundations. Named for the Clayoquot Indian tribe which once lived on its shores, the word means "people of a different or warlike nature." It was here that the Clayoquots displayed—atop tall poles driven into the white sands—the bloodied heads of their vanquished foes, the Kyuquots. Such were the trophies of the last battle, fought in 1855, between west coast native tribes. Even today, deep within natural caves on the outer beaches, Indian skeletons can still be seen, liberated from their graves by the relentless waves.

A small island, steeped in west coast history, Stubbs came to be the centre of trade and commerce in Clayoquot Sound. Its stewardship would pass through generations of settlers, come to make their fortunes in this oftentimes hostile environment. The store and post office serviced miners in search of gold in the surrounding mountains. They came to register their claims and purchase supplies. Whalers made frequent visits and sealing schooners stopped regularly to pick up cargoes of seal and (in earlier days) otter pelts, bound for the fashion conscious cities of Europe and Asia.

In the fall of 1987 I finally had a chance to visit Clayoquot with Rick, one of the local artists. The sturdy little wooden boat, newly christened *Popinjay* by its owner, left the private dock at ten o'clock on a hot sunny October morning and we made our way across the harbour. Strawberry Island lay to our starboard side and further on we passed the historic Indian village of Opitsaht, where the dwellings cast their reflections on the mirror-smooth surface of the ocean and the village cows grazed at the edge of the sea. Two dolphins began to frolic in the bow wave which seemed to me to be an auspicious beginning to the day. Rick tied up the boat at the former Government Dock and we made our way up the path to the lodge which sat deserted, in the midst of an emerald green lawn ringed by tall cedars.

The silence lay so heavy we felt like intruders, our voices seeming to hang in the still air. Rick looking, in his battered straw hat, much like Van Gogh, set out for the other side of the island to do some sketching. I began to wander slowly down the elongated spit of white sand that juts into the Sound like a pale finger. Fabled Lone Cone loomed across the water and Dream Isle lay close by. It was on this spit that the body of an enigmatic young Englishman had been discovered many years ago.

Madeline grew up on the small island, along with her four sisters and brothers. Her father, Clarence Dawley, bought Stubbs Island with its trading post around the turn of the century from a Danish seaman who had emigrated to Canada. (The Dane had married an Indian woman named Lucy, whose brother had badly beaten and left her for dead on the beach. Lucy gave birth to five children and died fifteen years later—poisoned by eating small mussels.) Beside the store and post office, there were a flourishing crab cannery, the school, a hotel, cabins built out on the sand spit, and even a small jail. Madeline remembers it as a busy place in those days. The general store served a large area and stocked everything from bolts of cloth to English soup plates, which, for some reason, were great favourites of the natives in the area. In early times, the natives made their purchases through a small wicket, and the storekeeper kept a loaded rifle nearby.

The family also sold groceries, including such things as twelve cooked crab for three dollars. In addition, Mr. Dawley had a prosperous sealskin business: he bought the pelts from the local Indians, salted them down, and shipped them to England. They were entirely self-sufficient, although Madeline describes the well water as the colour of tea, causing all their linens to turn beige over the years. Rainwater, always plentiful, was collected for most of their needs. They had cows, raised chickens and pigs, tended fruit trees and a large vegetable garden.

Madeline's mother Rose was born and raised in Los Angeles. She was blessed with a lovely singing voice and had performed on stage with her parents and four sisters from the time she was a young child. Rose missed the lights of the city and so eventually Clarence bought a home in Victoria. Thereafter, the family divided their time between the city and the island.

At one point it was deemed desirable to form a tennis club, and a regulation sized patch of grass behind the hotel was chosen as the site for the court. The residents worked together to level it and fence it off from the solitary bull which, while admittedly not considered dangerous, was not trusted to have much respect for any tennis court. Although the court itself never was entirely level, and stubborn patches of sand kept reappearing, periodically impeding the ball, never was there a more enthusiastic tennis club than this one perched on the edge of the Pacific. Indeed, at one time it boasted more than seventy members.

One of the biggest events of the year was the Clayoquot Sports Day, held on the May 24th. holiday. People arrived by boat from miles around and there were spirited competitions in broad jump, pole vaulting, the greased pole, and various water sports, including the upset canoe race. Heavy dug-out canoes, each with two paddlers, would race to a designated point offshore, marked by a buoy, at which point the canoe was rolled, its passengers scrambling back in and powering it to the finish line. The big event was the tug-o-war, held on the final afternoon, after which the celebrations ended with a dance.

The hotel at Clayoquot was the first in British Columbia to obtain a government liquor licence and licence #1 was proudly framed and hung over the bar. Then came the days of prohibition, a time that would test the west coasters' ingenuity to the utmost. It was a challenge they met willingly, some would even say enthusiastically, and with undreamed-of imagination. Coastal rum-runners arrived frequently, and the cargo was offloaded in dark of night and added to the hotel's liquid assets. And, of course, there were also government inspectors arriving frequently. No one today is quite sure how it was arranged but word of the inspector's imminent appearance was always flashed to those concerned at Clayoquot. Shortly thereafter there was frenzied activity, much of it concentrated in the woods beyond, and, by the time the eminent official set foot on the dock, Clayoquot was—to all but the most discerning eye—essentially DRY.

However, as it is with even the most sophisticated communication systems, there was the occasional lapse. The story is told of the arrival of a schooner whose cargo consisted mainly of "potent potables." No sooner had they tied up at the dock than the boat belonging to the provincial police arrived and tied up alongside them, its two-man crew heading directly for the hotel. Prevented from unloading the contraband, and fearful of a search, the resourceful captain of the schooner ordered the entire load placed in the cargo net and carefully lowered over the side into the water. The next morning, at the mercy of an unusually low tide, the ship's captain noted to his horror that the damaging evidence was in full view of anyone not legally blind. To his amazement however, the police (for whatever reason) appeared not to notice, and were soon underway.

Also present on the island was a tiny village of Japanese fishermen and their families. This vibrant community lent a richness to the fabric of island life. The Japanese were admittedly the best fishermen on the west coast. It wasn't unusual for the men to stop in at the hotel with a catch of fish, take over the kitchen for the evening, and cook up a sumptuous meal, fit for king or emperor. In general, however, the Japanese families, while on good terms with everyone on the island, kept largely to themselves and maintained their age-old traditions.

The only thing felt to be lacking was the presence of a teacher. Finally, in 1939, Mrs. Barr (whose husband Roy was in the army overseas) arrived with her six small children and, with the Japanese children, the numbers were sufficient to open the one-room school once more. Her son Ken remembers their arrival at the dock: "The whole village turned out to meet us. They picked up our bags and escorted us proudly to our new home. The small house (on the edge of the Japanese village) was freshly painted, inside and out and everything was spotless." Ken tells of a Huck Finn existence on the island, a time of freedom and adventure. His best friends were his Japanese school mates.

So it was that, after the attack on Pearl Harbour by Japan, on December 7th. 1941, the harsh edict of the Canadian government—to remove all Japanese Canadians from coastal areas to internment camps in the interior—fell with shock and bewilderment on these young carefree schoolchildren. Ken watched with tears in his eyes as his friends and their families left for Vancouver on the *Princess Maquinna*. The Japanese presence on the island was gone, it seemed, practically overnight. Thereafter, the island children attended school in Tofino, crossing in the tiny boat christened the *Bee Gee,* which doubled as the hotel water taxi.

Clayoquot 1930

At the age of ten, Madeline had been sent to boarding school at St. Ann's Academy for Girls in Victoria. The young girl hated it, having been used to the blessed freedom of her island home, and yearned for the day she could return. Upon graduation she happily accepted the invitation of her parents to assist them in the running of the hotel and store. She was also in charge of the records office where marriages, births, and deaths were registered. ("We called them matches, hatches, and dispatches.") Soon after, at the local dance, she met Pierre, a handsome Frenchman, whose family had settled on nearby Vargas Island.

Pierre was working at the crab cannery at the time and after their marriage the couple bought the island from her parents. They remained there until 1942, when they moved to Victoria. The stewardship of Stubbs Island then passed into the hands of two very proper English ladies who, over the years, became local legends.

Betty, a young widow, came to Clayoquot to help her brother Bill with the management of the hotel. She had formerly been the owner of a dance studio in Victoria, one which specialized in ball room dancing. When her husband died, she decided to get away from the city for a while. She came to the west coast for one summer of employment, fell in love with the area, and never left. Betty purchased the island from Madeline and Pierre (including the hotel, store, crab cannery, cabins and other buildings) for $11,000.00. The energetic little woman soon became known along the coast for her generosity and fair trading practices.

It was wartime, and having the only beer parlour—the more fashionable term "pub" had not yet entered the Canadian vocabulary—on the west coast of the island, the hotel at Clayoquot did a flourishing business. A few miles away, at Long Beach, the third largest air base in Canada had been carved out of the wilderness. It opened in 1942. It was felt by many in command that a Japanese landing on the nearby beaches was imminent. Pilings were driven into the sand and observation posts were hastily constructed along the coast. Each night everyone, military and civilian, observed the strict blackout regulations.

Until then, Clayoquot could be reached only by boat, but the resourceful military engineers quickly pushed a dirt road through the rainforest to Tofino and from there it was only a ten minute boat trip to the island. Every ten days the steamship *Princess Maquinna* sailed around the point, anchored at the dock, and off-loaded supplies. On boat days, young Ken earned his allowance by helping unload hotel supplies. They were placed on a push cart that ran on rails from the dock directly into the warehouse. There was a dirt basement built beneath the bar, where the beer was stored. Ken earned an additional twenty-five cents on summer evenings by passing up supplies to the bartender above.

Many a military man has fond memories of the beer parlour at Clayoquot and its feisty little proprietor. It was said of Betty that she "ruled by the tap." She welcomed them all, but at the first sign of boisterousness the tap was turned off and it would remain in that position (for EVERYONE) until the proper amount of decorum had returned. Ladies were seated on one side of the room and men remained firmly rooted on the other. A local man remembers that when they built the Royal Canadian Legion in Tofino, her first competition, Betty sent them a cash register and wished them well.

After the war, the men went home and life on the west coast returned to normal. The rainforest inexorably began to reclaim its own. Few traces of those turbulent times are left. Some of the military buildings were relocated to the villages of Ucluelet or Tofino and the original airstrip has been lengthened and repaved. An occasional observation post still peers blindly out to sea and after a winter storm, when the sands have shifted, the few remaining pilings reveal themselves. One lone building, a former barracks, still stands in the forest, its roof leaking, windows long gone, foundation covered in moss.

While business thrived under Betty's guidance, her accounting system left much to be desired. Receipts from the bar might be stuffed in a vase, proceeds from the dining room dropped in a drawer, and various other monies stuffed in various nooks and crannies.

Seven years after Betty purchased the island, her older sister Jo, also a widow, and a former professional dancer who had studied ballet in London, came to live at Clayoquot. Jo, while more reserved than Betty, was a woman of strong convictions. These were, at all times, tempered by a dry sense of humour and a graceful manner. During the late 1930s she had been active in the Chinese Medical Aid Program which bought supplies for Dr. Norman Bethune's team in China. Together the sisters shared the responsibilities and challenges of the hotel, which eventually became known as "the lodge." Fortunately, Jo had a head for figures and quickly set up an efficient book-keeping system. She also helped with the correspondence and stock taking. Her skill at fortune telling made her a popular figure at any social gathering.

Clayoquot Sound is in the centre of one of North America's busiest flyways for migrating ducks and geese and, over the years, the lodge became a haven for hunters. Both ladies became proficient with a shotgun. Once, having assured a newly arrived hunter of the wealth of game birds in the region, Betty woke the following morning to find him shooting away at her tame geese.

The sisters became known as the best cooks on the west coast. The menu at the lodge was always varied and the portions generous. Food would be brought to the table in attractive ceramic bowls and platters, much like eating at home. Featured were fluffy French omelettes, home-made bread, fresh churned butter, hearty soups and fish chowders. Clams, oysters, crab, and octopus were obtained locally. Other specialties were pork and chicken from the cooler, fish and chips, the fish having been caught offshore the same day, and fresh vegetables and herbs from the garden. Desserts, which were Betty's specialty, ranged from English trifle to pineapple upside-down cake and fresh fruit pies.

While it was Jo who originally suggested the planting of rhododendrons around the grounds, the garden eventually became Betty's preoccupation in life. Her happiest times were spent out of doors, planting and maintaining the formal gardens that surrounded the lodge, and she brooked no interference from anyone, human or otherwise. More than once the police constable was rousted out of bed to investigate a report of a winking light observed on the grounds, only to discover it was Betty, out hunting her constant nemesis, the lowly slug, by flashlight.

Jo created a tranquil forest garden behind the lodge, along the path that led to the back beach. It blended so beautifully with the surroundings it was difficult to distinguish between the hand of nature and her own. To this day, as one walks the trail that leads to the caves on the other side of the island, rhododendrons (including some very rare species) can be seen growing wild. The sisters saved all the stale beer (with its B vitamins) from the hotel for the rhododendrons. Their theories, no matter how unorthodox, must have worked, as the island contains many unusual species that are quietly growing much beyond the proportions ascribed to them in any botanical journal.

Although the ladies of Clayoquot became proficient with gun and clam shovel, and quite at home milking cows and making bread, they never forgot their roots. Precisely at four o'clock each afternoon, regardless of what was happening on the island, the bar was closed and the ladies sat down to a proper English tea. When they rowed over to attend the weekly dances in Tofino (one of their favourite outings) they both wore long skirts of fine wool or linen, high button lace blouses, and long white gloves.

Over the years, Betty and Jo continued to foster good relations among the varied cultures of Clayoquot Sound. Not only was the place abuzz on sports days but each year, two weeks before Christmas, Clayoquot hosted a dinner for the local natives living on Meares Island. Often, when the *Maquinna* called, the ladies would be guests of the captain for a midnight supper, served on snowy linen and eaten beneath sparkling chandeliers. It was generally assumed by interested residents of the village that the good captain had his eye on one of the sisters, although which one was never agreed upon.

In 1964, after twenty-two years on the island, Betty and Jo decided to sell Clayoquot. They moved across the water to Tofino, a distance of one mile, together with their right-hand man Freddy, son of the Danish sea captain who, years before, had run the trading post. They bought property (once again from Madeline and Pierre) at Uzatses Point, site of a large Indian midden, overlooking the inlet. By this time they also owned Strawberry Island in the centre of the harbour. They set about transforming it into a garden and it became a special retreat for them.

They levelled off the highest point, planted grass, surrounded it with brilliantly coloured rhododendrons, and terraced it down to the sea. It became a fairly common sight to see the sisters in their small skiff transporting large bushes, roots trailing in the water behind the boat, over to the small island. A family of eagles had a nest in the tall cedars that grew in the centre of the island. Often on a summer afternoon the ladies would row over to have tea, their vantage point affording them a spectacular view of Lemmens Inlet ringed by mountains. Jo's daughter Mary tells of the day they were enjoying themselves so much they left the island later than planned and their little boat was swept through the gap on the strong incoming tide. Luckily Mary spied them from the shore and a friend was dispatched with his motor boat to effect a rescue. Both sisters lived to a fine old age on their beloved west coast and their graves have been lovingly enhanced with miniature species of the plants they both loved.

As the years passed, Clayoquot came to know many stewards. Some it embraced, others it merely endured. Most recently, for a few years, Dorothy and her husband Al experienced the island and its many charms. Once again the island became a centre of west coast hospitality. One of Dorothy's most poignant memories of the island is the distinct impression of the presence of a ghost—a gentle, most endearing "little person." She describes it as child-size, with an undoubtedly brown face. Records reveal that a Japanese child from Clayoquot was drowned at sea while fishing with his father in the 1930s. The father, unable to cope with the tragedy, eventually committed suicide. The presence was often perceived by Dorothy as she sat at her desk, doing the accounts. Whenever she attempted to confront it, the small ghost would move on, disappearing around a corner or up the stairs. Curiously, Dorothy was not the only one to be aware of the waif-like entity; it has appeared to several women over the years, although no man has ever mentioned seeing it.

And so, that day on the Clayoquot sand spit, it wasn't difficult to imagine I heard voices from the past or saw the sealing schooners standing off-shore. As I slowly retraced my steps along the edge of the water, I noticed large moon-snail shells being gently tumbled onto the shore by the waves. There were many others at the high tide line, already bleached white by the sun. I gathered them up and placed them in my cotton bag, as tangible reminders of this very special day.

I met Rick coming along the overgrown path through the trees and together we climbed the stairs of the old lodge and peered through the windows. All was in perfect order, as if the kitchen doors would swing wide at any moment and Betty and Jo would emerge to sit down to afternoon tea. We walked across the emerald tennis court of yesteryear and made our way down the path to the dock. A noisy little seaplane droned overhead as it came in for a landing, pulling our thoughts back to modern-day reality.

THREE

Ladies of Long Beach

There are many "long beaches" on the west coast of Vancouver Island. Crescents of pristine white sand alternately lapped and pounded by the green waters of the Pacific ocean. Most, however, are accessible only by float plane or boat and have rarely known the presence of man. It is the beach that lies within the perimeters of Pacific Rim National Park, between the sister villages of Ucluelet and Tofino, that has become known and loved by people the world over.

In early times, in the spring of the year, when days grew longer, when herring spawn caused the waters to turn milky and the great whales could be glimpsed in the outer waters on their spring migration to northern latitudes, the Clayoquot tribe left their principal village of Opitsaht on the shores of Meares Island and travelled by war canoe to their summer camp on Wickaninnish Bay, today known as Long Beach. While the women and children tended camp the men hunted and fished in the time honored ways of their forefathers and stood ready to defend their territory from all enemies, most notably the Makahs under Chief Tatoosh from Cape Flattery to the south. Today, near the ancient ruins, stand a cliff-face covered with petroglyphs and a burial ground, mute tributes to the original stewards of Long Beach.

Next came the settlers, most from Europe, lured by the promise of free land and an unfettered life on the rugged Canadian west coast. They staked out pre-emptions and set about earning a living in the burgeoning logging, mining, and fishing industries. Later, occasional intrepid travellers discovered the bonanza of white sand beaches and pounding surf beyond the snow-clad mountains, and went home to spread the word. At that point some of the more enterprising settlers began to build cottages to accommodate those in search of lodging and the foundation was laid for today's flourishing tourist trade.

It was here, in Clayoquot Sound, that Hazel, born in 1901, spent her childhood. Her parents travelled west as missionaries around the turn of the century. Sam was twenty-one, Christena only fifteen, when, soon after their marriage, they renounced the comforts of small town Ontario to bring the word of God to the west coast Indians. They settled first in Clo-oose, moving later to an island in the Sound, purchased for them by Christena's parents.

Christena's island home was a sturdy little log cabin. To keep out the winter drafts, she papered the walls with pages from religious magazines. This served the dual purpose of insulating and providing inspirational reading material. While Sam tended to the spiritual needs of the natives, Christena worked among the native women, holding Bible classes and serving as mid-wife.

She was also wise enough to learn from them and adapt to many of the older, traditional ways. She became expert at spearing fish from the shore and in the spring, when the herring spawned, she gathered the eggs laid on eel grass in the shallow waters. These she dried, along with herbs of the area, for use in stews and chowders. She also began to use the local herbs for medicinal purposes.

Sam set up a Methodist mission with funds sent from back east and worked among the natives of the area. A large portion of his time was spent lecturing against the evils of "demon rum" which—introduced by early fur traders—was decimating the Indian population.

Four sons and two daughters were born to the couple. One son died at the age of four after suffering a high fever and convulsions. The young parents laid him out, read a simple service, and buried their beloved child in a plot of ground close to the house in a small, hand-hewn coffin. The children attended school in Tofino. In good weather they rowed across the harbour each day but once the winter storms set in, they remained at home, where they were taught by Christena. When Hazel was fifteen, the family moved to Port Alberni. By then funds for the mission had run out, and Sam and his sons set up a mail and passenger service running between Bamfield and points north. Their first boat was the thirty-five foot merchant vessel *Tofino*.

Hazel's first love was music and she dreamed of becoming a concert pianist, but eventually surrendered the dream to become one of the first wireless telegraphers in Vancouver, call number VE5AF. She was a handsome young woman and her company was eagerly sought. In the course of several years she was engaged to be married a total of seven times. "Somehow, when it came to actually setting the date, I couldn't go through with it, but I always returned the ring."

Hazel's brother Stuart became captain of the *Malahat*, a five-masted auxiliary schooner, length 245 feet, breadth 43 feet and depth 23 feet. She was built in Victoria in 1917, originally for the Australian lumber trade. By the time Stuart assumed command, the *Malahat* was serving as mother ship during the lucrative rum-running years on the coast during the years of prohibition in the United States. From 1924 to 1933, when Congress repealed the Volstead Act, the *Malahat* was one of the most wanted ships on the California coast. She could hold sixty thousand cases of liquor, with a cash value of over one million dollars. Loaded in Vancouver, she would make a run for California where she lay just inside international waters, enabling buyer's vessels to approach without fear of confrontation with authorities. She was crewed by expert mariners but another secret of her success was the close communication maintained between the captain of the vessel and the wireless operators back in Vancouver. These women broadcast the location of all ships in the area in a carefully constructed code, making the apprehension of the Canadian ship nearly impossible. They were exciting years and money earned working aboard the rum-runner feathered many a west coaster's nest. The *Malahat* ended her days as a log carrier, working mostly in the Queen Charlotte Islands. She was swamped off Cape Beale in 1944 and today lies submerged in Barkley Sound.

One day Stuart introduced Hazel to Jim, his red-headed first mate and good friend, and quietly told Hazel later that she was a fool if she didn't marry him. Within a short time brother Stuart learned, to his delight, that it had been love at first sight for the couple. Jim was a fine and gentle man, with the soul of an artist, twenty-one years Hazel's senior. Previously he had spent many years serving as first mate aboard trading ships on the Hawaiian run. After a courtship lasting three years, Hazel, the daughter of missionaries, and Jim, the Irish rum-runner, were married. It was a long and loving relationship.

In 1932 Jim and Hazel moved back to the west coast. Their first home was a large tent, (16'x 22') with a wooden floor, that they erected on the sands at Long Beach. They lived in the tent for four years, until they bought property and began to build cabins. Hazel remembers those years in the tent on the beach as the happiest of their married lives. "The floor would vibrate from the pounding surf and the deer used to poke their heads through the tent flap when I was cooking." There were also cougars and bears in the area but all the inhabitants of the beach lived in harmony with one another. They were good years, with every aspect of daily living governed by tides and the vagaries of the weather. Perhaps the charm and simplicity of those early days on Long Beach are best captured in an excerpt from Jim's journal in which, in the best tradition of a sea-going man, he recorded the small events that made up their days.

15 August 1933   Sunrise 6:06 A.M. Sunset 8:31 P.M. Low Tide 10:14 A.M. High Tide 4:10 P.M. Overcast with light chop. Wind west by northwest 12 knots.

Rose at 6:30 A.M. After breakfast, worked on boat (repairing keel). Then, while Hazel baked bread, I went clam digging. Got one pailful (16), also raked in two crabs. Came across large cedar log (3 feet diameter) that washed in during the night, secured it. Mary and Art walked out from Ucluelet and stayed for lunch (crabs and bread). After lunch the four of us walked back to the log and managed to float it down to our site. At high tide we pulled it up on the beach and secured it with ropes to the boom. After supper (Shipwreck salad, clams, bread, plum crisp and coffee), we played a game of croquet and then Mary and Art caught a ride back to town in Hillier's truck. Sunset particularly beautiful tonight, gold to crimson, water stained pink. Hazel made popcorn and I began work on plans for the house while she made out an order for Eaton's catalogue. Retired 10:30 P.M.

Other excerpts speak of breaking the sod for their first house, followed a few months later with the decision to erect four cabins. Every structure would be built from driftwood cast up on the beach. Later, Jim recorded the name chosen for their small resort—Camp Maquinna—in honour of the chief of the Nootkas. Hazel still treasures the scuffed leather journals.

Christena and Sam both lived to a healthy old age in Port Alberni and seemed to mellow as the years passed. At the age of forty, Christena took up dancing (even though she had injured her knee in a fall from the dock, and ever after walked with a limp) and playing cards and even began to make wine from the many berries of the area. Although no one in the household ever imbibed "fermented spirits," she maintained that she liked to have it on hand to offer to visitors. No visitor ever had the heart to tell Christena that it was probably the worst tasting wine they had ever experienced.

After many years of providing accommodation on the beach, Jim and Hazel retired to Victoria, and continued to live within sight and smell and sound of the ocean. Jim died at the age of ninety and Hazel remains active twenty years later also at the age of ninety. She recently gave up smoking and driving her Mercedes but continues to travel with friends to points as distant as Hawaii and Japan.

Early visitors to the west coast were—by all accounts—a fine type of tourist. The area attracted naturalists and artists, biologists and photographers, along with those who simply wanted to observe the forces of nature in a quiet and peaceful environment. Among the artists who visited were Emily Carr—named "Klee Wyck" or "Laughing One" by the Indians of Ucluelet and the shy young Arthur Lismer, who later became a founding member of the illustrious "Group of Seven."

In those days (as it is today), one of the favourite occupations of anyone who walked the long white sands of Wickaninnish Bay was beachcombing. Everything from cooking utensils, life preservers, and steamer trunks (most of it flotsam from various shipwrecks), to other, more deadly objects, washed in on the wayward waves.

Highly prized were the glass floats of various shapes and sizes: from large clear balls, some of them two feet in diameter, to smaller brown, cigar-shaped cylinders. These floats had originally escaped from Japanese fishing nets and bobbed their way across thousands of miles of non-pacific seas to tumble, with delightful frequency, upon the accommodating sands of the new world. Some were encrusted with barnacles, proof of a journey of several years. Today they have become collector's items, as the modern Japanese fishing fleets turn increasingly to styrofoam and plastic.

A short distance down the beach stood another resort, one that would become synonymous with the years of transition—some would say dissolution—on the beach. "Singing Sands" became a haven for many of the disenchanted youth of the sixties, who travelled to the west coast from all points of North America, and sometimes beyond. They came—seeking answers to questions they weren't even sure they understood.

Owner, and guiding spirit of this establishment, was a friendly little widow who came to be loved and respected by all the young people who found sanctuary on the beach. Peg was born in England in 1905, and her family emigrated to Canada in 1910, bound for Victoria. Upon arrival, they lived for three months in the recently constructed Empress Hotel until their new home was finished. They lived in Cadboro Bay, at Ten Mile Point, and Peg and her brother attended classes in a small one-room school. Upon graduation, she became a fencing instructor, and spent several years teaching the sport in southern California. Upon returning to Victoria she met Dick, her brother's best friend, and a skilled lens grinder. They were married in 1935.

Soon after, Dick hiked from Port Alberni to Long Beach. "It had such unspoiled beauty in those days. At a time when the rest of the country was mired in the depression, here was a place where a person could practically live off the land." When he returned, they decided to move, and travelled up the coast aboard the mail boat *Victory* to Ucluelet where they were taken by truck to Long Beach.

They bought the original Tibbs property located on the beach in 1936. Tibbs, a young Englishman, had relocated to a small island (Dream Isle) in the Tofino harbour several years earlier, where he quickly became part of the local folklore. The old cabin that came with the property sat on the brow of a hill overlooking the beach. The structure, windows missing, front porch sagging leaned at an alarming angle but fortunately the roof didn't leak. The first thing the young couple did was build a shed for their provisions, next they set about clearing their land. It was hard work. Up at first light, they worked every day until dark. Their luck held: it didn't rain that year until after Christmas. However, that also meant they had to haul their water from the creek, half a mile away.

Their next project was to build their first home from the piles of driftwood thrown up daily onto the beach. Despite uncertain weather conditions, rather primitive tools, and the fact that neither had held a hammer before, it became a labour of love. Within a few months their sturdy little shake-roofed house had been constructed for the grand total of seventy-five dollars. During the winter they walked to Tofino for supplies and mail, using the trail cut through the dense rainforest and timing their trips to coincide with the regular arrival of the steamship. At a good pace their trip took three hours. In summer they travelled by small boat along the inside passage, taking a picnic lunch and making a day of it. Next, they began to build small cottages amongst the tall pine trees. They eventually had nine. "Singing Sands," the name they chose, aptly described the natural phenomenon that they experienced every day as the waves hit the beach.

After several years, war broke out and Dick became one of the first surveyors for the Long Beach airport, to be built on North Long Beach, a short distance from their property. In addition to the airport, a military seaplane base was quickly established in Ucluelet.

In the months following the surprise attack on Pearl Harbour, there was thought to be a very real possibility of a Japanese landing on the hitherto peaceful beaches of the Canadian west coast. Watch towers were hastily constructed on promontories, barbed wire was strung along the beach, and machine guns were installed, their ugly snouts pointing toward the land of the rising sun.

Con Smythe—one of Canada's most beloved bush pilots—flew in as commander of an early squadron. The men were billeted in tents set up in an area known as Lovekins Meadow. That first year the rains never seemed to let up. The meadow flooded regularly, and, because of floating beds, wood stoves that refused to light, and clothes that never felt dry, the men quickly dubbed it "Operation Sponge." Local fishermen, anxious to aid in the war effort, formed the "Gum Boot Navy" and helped patrol the local waters. This informal band of protectors earned the respect and gratitude of the military and fellow west coasters alike.

Many of the military wives were allowed to accompany their husbands, and some were lucky enough to find accommodation at "Singing Sands," where Peg and Dick promptly took them under their wings. All women in the Long Beach area were directed to have small bundles of food and clothing ready, in case of evacuation. The plan was to drive them to Kennedy Lake, cross by boat, and then hike out over the old telegraph trail to Port Alberni. Later, when Estevan Point was shelled by a submarine, the military wives were flown to Vancouver for a period of several weeks. Other west coast women refused to go.

Perhaps because it was wartime, a spirit of camaraderie prevailed. Regularly invited to the officers' mess as guests of the commanding officer, Peg and Dick played bridge and danced to the music of Glenn Miller. "There was a pervasive feeling of all being in the same boat, so to speak. In many ways those were good years, years that provoke nostalgia in anyone living through those times." After the war the west coast slowly returned to normalcy, with few traces of those turbulent years remaining.

Tragically, in 1948, Dick lost his life in the waters off his beloved beach. Early one morning as he worked on the roof of the cabin he was building, he spied a mine, remnant of the war, resting on the sands, at the high tide line. He contacted the Coast Guard in Ucluelet and they immediately dispatched the life boat with crew, to disarm the deadly object. The men succeeded in

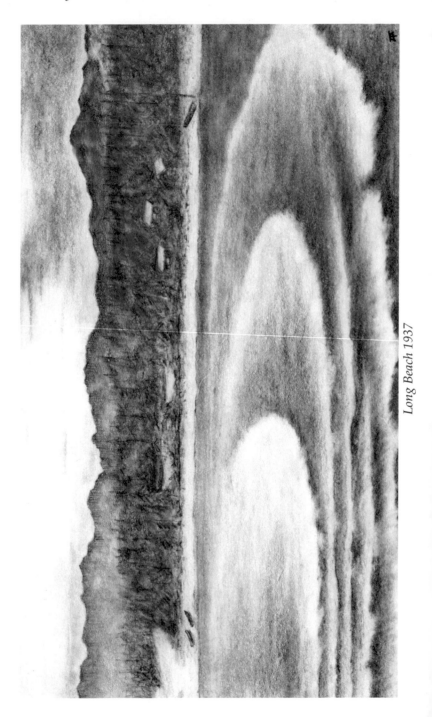

Long Beach 1937

safely dismantling the explosive but encountered heavy seas as they sought to leave. In the frantic struggle to free the boat from the reef, Dick drowned before Peg's eyes (as did one of the crew of the lifeboat). From that time on, Peg was alone.

She continued to operate "Singing Sands," catering to visitors who would arrive in Ucluelet by boat, then hire a truck to take them out to the beach. Often, if Peg knew they were coming, she would meet them up on the trail with her pony (Bouquet) and cart.

Every ten days Peg sent out a grocery order to Victoria, and an excerpt from a yellowed bill of sale reflects the cost of living of that time:

Canadian Beauty Noodles	3 boxes...............	25c
Campbells Tomato Soup	6 tins	66c
Dole Pineapple Chunks	4 tins	72c
Knox Gelatin	3 pkg.	66c
Mazola Corn Oil	1 quart	1.60c
Island Butter	3 tins	1.35c
Brown Rice	6 lbs.	33c
Salada Tea	4 lbs.	1.96c
Southern Pride Raisins	2 lbs.	28c
Nabob Coffee	3 lbs.	1.30c
Peanut Butter	1 lb.	48c

These staples, along with other necessities of life, were purchased in the grocery section of the Hudson's Bay department store in Victoria. There they were carefully packed in boxes and delivered by truck to the steamship *Princess Maquinna,* berthed in the Inner Harbour. From there they enjoyed a leisurely cruise north to Ucluelet, where they were promptly unloaded onto a rickety delivery truck and sent over the goat trail that passed for a road, to arrive at Peg's back door at "Singing Sands." At that point, she gladly paid the shipping charge of ten cents, fed the delivery man lunch, and tipped him a shiny nickle.

In 1959 an event occurred that would alter forever the fragile illusion of splendid isolation that west coasters had enjoyed until then. On the morning of August twenty-second, a caravan, composed of seventy-five cars, drove over the newly constructed road from Port Alberni to the west coast. This avenue of commerce, much of it high in the clouds, had long been petitioned for by west coasters and was jointly funded by the provincial government and logging companies working in the area. Though it was basically a logging road, pot-holed and hair-pin turned, it functioned as a link to the outside world—that larger part of the universe loosely termed by those residing on the far side of the mountains as civilization.

As one old timer put it, "The day the ROAD opened, it forced us, some kicking and bellyaching, into the twentieth century." A trip that formerly took half a day, could now be accomplished in two hours—not accounting for flat tires and broken axles. From that time on, the west coast was accessible to anyone in possession of a driver's licence or a jauntily cocked thumb.

The road ushered in an era that would—in its own way—alter and polarize large segments of west coasters in directions probably never envisioned by the early pioneers. A migration to the west coast of the island began. The stream, at first a trickle, which grew to a flood, was composed of young people, many from the United States, who had begun to question the traditional values and mores. They demonstrated mounting resistance to graphic examples of man's inhumanity to man, most notably the war in Viet Nam: the first war in history to be displayed on the television screens of the nation every night. Many young men crossed Canada's borders to escape the draft, other idealists followed, seeking solace in a country not actively at war. Dubbed "flower children" by the media of the time, a term that still endures, they spawned ideas and loyalties that would alter forever the "status quo."

Housed in lean-tos constructed of driftwood and tarpaulins, they lived on the Florencia Bay section of Long Beach, named for a barquentine wrecked there in 1861. Years ago prospectors had worked the sands for fine gold. The numbers of these modern young beach dwellers eventually grew to such proportions that Statistics Canada assigned a census taker to the area, also known as Wreck Bay, in an effort to bring this amorphous group of free spirits under the umbrella of federal stewardship.

Many of the newcomers were well educated, creative young people who simply chose to opt out of the mainstream of society. This, at a time when even the most ardent traditionalists were beginning to question, no matter how tentatively, long held beliefs. Some were unkempt, refugees from the "cleanliness is next to Godliness" generation. Because of this fact, together with their long hair, psychedelic tones of dress and use of marijuana, these prophets of the future immediately cast a negative image, shadows of which linger today.

Peg was one of the few people of her generation to accept these beach dwellers, known to this day, by some, as hippies. As time went on, she became actively involved in their lives. Many referred to her affectionately as "The Godmother." She rented her cabins to them, became their friend and spiritual advisor, and more than once underwrote a loan.

"On Friday nights when I played bridge with the neighbours, the young people would come to my home to bake (I had the only wood-burning stove). They always cleaned up after themselves and left me a loaf of bread, or topped off the cookie jar. Whenever I was away, they kept an eye on things—collected the rents, weeded the garden, and fed the ponies. Looking back, I think of those years and the people they embraced as the most meaningful of my life. Many of them left, and are now working within the establishment, but not necessarily in the established way. Others stayed, settled in the area, and are now making a real contribution to the west coast."

Then suddenly—with the stroke of a pen—the lifestyles and livelihoods of those who called Long Beach their home, were irrevocably altered. In 1970, the area was designated as Pacific Rim, Canada's newest national park, and large parcels of land were expropriated. Much of it had been held by the C.P.R., who, before the first World War, had contemplated laying a rail line out to the coast. Other lots were held by absentee landlords and speculators who had never seen or experienced the west coast. Most of these people jumped at the chance to sell their land.

Fifty-six families, owners of resorts, small shops, and galleries were forced to relocate, including Peg. "Of course the government paid us market value for the actual land, but how could they recompense us for a lifestyle? I was offered a job in the national parks bureaucracy but turned it down. I really doubt that the government could have co-existed with me." In 1970 the Trans-Canada Highway was extended from Port Alberni to the coast. Once the lower, black-topped route was established, the logging road was abandoned to the eagles.

Peg lives today in a comfortable home close to the ocean in Victoria. She has a large extended family composed of the former young people of the beach and their families. Her cosy living room is bedecked with pictures of her "kids" and their offspring. It is rare to find her at home alone because now the second generation is finding safe haven with "The Godmother." And so the cycle continues.

Nowadays the pulse of life on the west coast moves in an approximate rhythm with the rest of the island, with only the occasional irregular beat. Most of the homes of the pioneers have been slowly consumed by the rainforest, and traces of the war years are few. The more things change however, the more they stay the same. The area still attracts artists, adventurers, and philosophers, as well as the new breed, the environmentalists.

In recent months, a project (which is still in the developmental stage), when completed, will bring the history of the Long Beach area full circle. Descendants of one of the original Clayoquot Sound Indian tribes, the Tla-o-qui-aht First Nations, plan to build a traditional native tourist resort, the first of its kind in the region. The focus of the resort will be to reflect the values of their people and will offer indigenous native foods and activities. It is hoped the concept will further good relations among white people and the original inhabitants of "the beach."

FOUR

Dream Isle

Trondheim, Norway, 1896. The sturdy young woman stood at the rail of the large, three-masted packet ship as it made its way majestically down the green-clad fjord. The sails quickened and swelled as the ship plunged into the cold grey waters of the north Atlantic. Johanna was bundled in furs, her golden braids hidden, her rosy cheeks and blue eyes barely visible above the knitted scarf. The parting from her family had been emotional. When, if ever, would she see her parents again?

At the age of twenty, Johanna was bound for Canada to marry Jacob, her childhood sweetheart, who had gone ahead four years previously to establish a foothold in the new world. Down below, in the hold of the ship, were the wooden trunks containing her trousseau. The most important item would prove to be the small Fabrik-Marke sewing machine, given to her by her mother. After a seventeen-day voyage, the young woman disembarked in Montreal and travelled by train across Canada. Jacob met her in Victoria where they were married the following day. Immediately after the wedding they left for the west coast of Vancouver Island aboard the steamship *Tees*.

In the years to follow, Jacob's four brothers also emigrated to the west coast and together they founded a fishing dynasty. These young Norwegian fishermen were among the first to realize what potential there was for a commercial salmon fishing industry in the rich waters off British Columbia. The brothers all married and raised families and at one time almost every second person in the small village of Tofino was of Norwegian extraction.

In those days, in an attempt to begin to settle the west, the Canadian government advertised free land, in parcels known as preemptions. Ads were placed in overseas papers and posters appeared in the streets of large European cities. Immigrants from Northern Europe (where owning land was becoming an impossible dream) began to arrive on our shores. However, the newcomers soon realized that the information had been misleading. The land was beautiful and much of it was as fertile as had been described, but the posters neglected to mention that the land had to be cleared by hand, roads needed to be built, and schools did not exist. Few of the would-be settlers had envisioned the intimidating isolation and the loneliness.

A man could file for two hundred acres and when he had built a home the property was his. The only requirement was the payment of taxes. Many stayed, despite the conditions, and built their homesteads. Others, finding their land to be swampy and unproductive, unable even to support cattle, were forced to return home, penniless and disillusioned.

Jacob's pre-emption was located on Grice Bay (today the site of the Long Beach airport) on rich mud flats, where the waters offered up a bounteous harvest and the land needed only to be tamed. Over the next few years, Jacob and Johanna worked together, clearing their land which was jungle-like rainforest, building a home, and raising a family.

Alma, the first of their seven children and their only daughter, was born in 1897. In the succeeding years, Johanna would give birth to six sons. Winters were spent on the homestead, which eventually boasted a well, vegetable garden, and fruit trees. The family had two cows, and fish, ducks, and deer were plentiful. During the summer months the family would relocate to the summer fishing grounds further up the inlet, at a place called Cannery Bay. Several other families did the same. Alma recalls it as much like one long camping trip and it was a happy time, particularly for the children.

As a child, Alma was sometimes allowed, as a special treat, to accompany her father on one of his infrequent trips to the settlement of Clayoquot, on Stubbs Island, several miles down the inlet. They would choose a calm day and leave on the early morning tide, keeping a sharp eye out for any change in the weather. In those days it was all sail and oar, as the gas engine did not arrive until 1910.

Alma loved those trips down the inlet: "It seemed as if there were no one in the world except my father and me. Mother always packed us a lunch and sometimes my father would allow me to help him row the boat. One time a school of dolphins followed us most of the way." Once at Clayoquot, they would purchase the supplies that Johanna had carefully listed. The storekeeper, Mr. Dawley, always had a little surprise for Alma—hard candy, nuts, or a pencil. Later, while Jacob chatted with the other fishermen, Alma would visit with Madeline, the storekeeper's daughter. They would often play on the beach and watch as whalers set sail for the Orient or sealing schooners were loaded with bales of skins. In later years, treaties were passed, forbidding such harvests. Finally, after loading the boat, Jacob and his small daughter would row home.

It was a struggle for Johanna and Jacob to provide for their large family but Alma remembers the home was spotless, the meals hearty, and practically every piece of clothing was fashioned on the trusty little sewing machine from across the sea. At Christmas, the children would accompany their father out into the forest to cut down a small tree. There were always cocoa and fresh baked cookies waiting for them when they got home. They would place the tree on the table in the parlour and decorate it with strings of popcorn and handmade ornaments. Mr. Dawley made up Christmas boxes for each family in the area. These contained sections filled with various types of fruit and nuts. One year there was a fresh orange for each of the children, their first, and another time the box contained a porcelain doll for Alma and small wooden boats for the boys.

Alma and her six brothers attended school in Tofino, in a small one-room building down on the waterfront, next to the general store. As the boys grew older they began fishing with their father and uncles, and eventually became skippers of their own boats.

Alma was of great help to her mother, assisting her with the cooking, sewing, and gardening. Music was always an important part of Alma's life. It was a proud day when the family finally obtained a piano. It was ordered through the Hudson's Bay Company in Victoria and shipped north on the *Princess Maquinna* soon after that venerable ship came into service. Unloaded at Clayoquot, the precious instrument was then transferred to a scow for the remainder of the journey up the inlet.

Both parents were anxious for their daughter to further her education and so, upon her finishing high school, it was decided that Alma would attend business school for a year in Tacoma, Washington. She took secretarial courses and received her diploma as stenographer. After graduation, she returned to work in Victoria for several months.

In 1916, she returned to Tofino to act as bridesmaid for a former classmate. Once home, she made the decision to resign from her job in the city and return to Tofino to assist her parents. By then her father was manager of the sawmill at Mosquito Harbour, the largest cedar lumber mill on the Pacific coast at that time. For the rest of his life Jacob figured prominently in the affairs of the small municipality, including serving as its first mayor.

Alma and Jacob

Being a man of vision, he campaigned tirelessly, along with others, for a road into the area but didn't see it within his lifetime. Alma became his bookkeeper and stenographer.

In later years Jacob bought property in the village itself and built a large home overlooking the harbour. From that time on, Johanna delighted in watching her sons return safely home from a day at sea. The original homestead on Grice Bay stood for many years, although no traces remain today. Remnants of the domestic herd roamed wild long after the family left, providing beef for anyone prepared to hunt them.

By then much of the settlement and trade had begun to shift from Clayoquot to the mainland and the former trading post eventually became largely a tourist destination. Once war broke out, the men of the outer islands left, practically en masse, to volunteer, and many of their families relocated to the village of Tofino. The young people of the area enjoyed a lively social life. Much of it centered around the church, weekly dances in the community hall, and parties held in the homes. Someone in the village, upon returning from the city, brought with him the first phonograph seen on the west coast. It was equipped with round cylinder records. Later, they had a gramophone with small wax records.

St. Columba church was constructed in 1913 and named for a sixth century Irish missionary. It was built with funds bequeathed to the presbytery by a couple in Portsmouth, England. They requested a church be built to honor the memory of their son, a young sailor lost at sea. The only condition stipulated that it be constructed on the prettiest spot on the west coast. And so, the little red cedar church rose on a point overlooking the inlet and Meares Island. The church became an integral part of the family's life.

It was during these years that Alma met a young Englishman, distant cousin of Robert Browning, and their bittersweet romance became part of the folklore of the west coast. Fred Tibbs arrived from England in 1910 and pre-empted property on Long Beach, where today the government has established a campground. After several years he sold this property and bought a small island in the Tofino harbour, facing the village. He promptly set about transforming a piece of Canadian wilderness into a little patch of England.

He christened it "Dream Isle" and built a lovely home (known locally as "The Castle"), with crenelated watch tower. He painted it white, with red and blue trim, and surrounded it with a typically English flower garden. The only thing missing was a princess in the tower, so he painted a picture of this princess and put it in the window facing west. Next, he cut down most of the trees except for one tall spruce in the centre, which he topped at one hundred feet. He built a ladder, attaching the rungs to the trunk of the tree and enclosing them with an outer frame for safety. On the top he constructed a small platform, from which vantage point he could see for miles. To the amazement of the townspeople, who, with varying degrees of curiosity, had observed his efforts over the months, he then began to level off a bicycle track around the perimeter of the island.

He soon became a favourite of the young women of the district, being in great demand at the local dances and picnics. Because of an accident as a child, he had deep dimples on the left side of his face, and this fact seemed only to increase his air of mystery. He was a shy and sensitive young man, who, nevertheless, enjoyed a good time.

He was a gifted musician, had a lovely singing voice, and owned a large collection of records. Each morning, at eight o'clock sharp, he played "Come to the Cookhouse Door, Boys" on his gramophone. He also wrote poetry, which he included in his letters to his young nieces in England. Often, on warm summer evenings, he would climb to his platform in the air and play his cornet. From his perch, over one hundred feet above the ground, he could see for miles up the Sound in every direction, including Dead Mans Isle nearby, where the natives of the area hung their dead in the branches of tall spruce trees.

The music wafted across the water from the island to the village, leading its good citizens to speculate about whom he was serenading. There were two young women listening with special interest, for each knew in her heart that the music was for her.

Tibbs worked at odd jobs and when an opportunity came to be part of the construction crew that was to build the lighthouse at Triangle Island, off the northern tip of Vancouver Island in 1910, he accepted. The island was desolate, swept by gales, its only inhabitants being sea birds. He wrote of his loneliness there and requested Mr. Dawley to send him a "mouth harp."

Years later he was appointed to tend the lights in the Tofino harbour. He had a small skiff, *Agnes,* equipped with one of the new gas engines. In those days the lights consisted of coal-oil lamps set in tripods atop large, flat-bottomed wooden floats. Every second day he was required to visit each of the lights in the harbour, leave a new lamp, and take the old one home for refilling.

Sometime in the early morning of July 5, 1921, Tibbs serviced the first light and then went out to the far one, off Mission Point. He was in the habit of merely pulling the prow of the skiff up over the wooden platform while he worked on the light. This morning, the motion of the ebbing tide caused the boat to slip off the float and it began to drift away. Tibbs was a strong swimmer and prepared to go after it. He stripped and carefully hung his clothes on the tripod. Then he entered the water which was always frigid, even in mid-summer.

A stiff breeze had sprung up, and the combination of wind and tide soon pulled the boat beyond any hope of retrieval. By the time Tibbs realized this and turned for shore, he was rapidly tiring. At this point he began battling thick beds of kelp whose slippery arms reached out to fasten him in their embrace, and the deadly effects of hypothermia.

He finally reached the sand spit on Stubbs Island, exhausted, with barely enough strength to pull himself out of the water. He collapsed and died there on the white sand, within hailing distance of the sleeping settlement of Clayoquot. His body was found a short time later, when the village began to stir.

Could this modest young man, whose quiet demeanor served to conceal a passionate nature, have had some presentiment of his fate? In a letter written to his niece in England shortly before his death, he included one of his many poems:

When Noah Entered the Ark

> *When at length on a mountain's crest*
> *Noah's ark on the dry came to rest*
> *It dawned on him that there was missing a rat*
> *For freedom contriving*
> *He started by diving*
> *And lastly to swim*
> *Determined and grim*
> *But simply went around*
> *Till exhausted he drowned*
> *Being finally found*
> *By his death bubbles crowned.*

Tibbs' body was interred in the cemetery on Morpheus Island in the Sound.

Next came the reading of his will, one that shocked all who thought they knew him yet never suspected the depth of his feelings. In it he left Dream Isle to Alma, ("because she's the nicest girl I ever met, and another reason she knows") and everything thereon, EXCEPTING, the house and ten feet of land on all sides. The house, and contents thereof, except the gramophone, was left to Olive, another winsome young lady of the village, and daughter of the lighthouse keeper ("because it was built for her"). The two young women were good friends and the matter was amicably resolved.

Alma bought the house from her friend and shortly thereafter sold island and house to the local fisheries officer. This gentleman was subsequently murdered on the island (word had it that he was bootlegging to the Indians) and for years afterward the island was shunned by the local people. Today, Tibbs Island is clad in the bright green of second growth forest, one of the loveliest in the Sound. However, often after the sun goes down, wolves can be heard howling on the island and the sound can raise the hair on one's neck.

Two years later, in 1923, Alma married Harold, son of the local store keeper in Tofino. Theirs was a happy and fruitful marriage. Harold had served overseas, his battalion having fought in France at Ypres and Mons. Upon his return he bought a troller, *The Violet,* and fished for several years. Later the young couple moved to Courtenay where Harold and a partner purchased two seven-passenger Hudson cars and ran a stage line between Courtenay and Nanaimo. Eventually they bought a bus. A few years later they sold out to B.C. Electric and moved to Victoria. Harold ran an oil station directly across from the Hudson's Bay Company.

Their comfortable home became a natural stopping place for west coast fishermen who came to Victoria to sell their catch and pick up supplies. With all this contact, the couple became homesick for the coast and, after four years, sold their home and car and returned to Tofino. Alma's parents gave them a piece of property in town and they built a sturdy home. By this time they had a daughter Marjorie, aged six, and son Raymond, four.

Harold fished with one of Alma's uncles. Eventually he gave up fishing and worked as engineer at the life boat station. He remained there until his death in 1957. Raymond died at sea in 1969, and daughter Marjorie, who married the purser on the *Princess Maquinna,* lives in Victoria.

Today, at the age of ninety-three, Alma lives alone in her home by the sea. Johanna and Jacob lie buried on Morpheus Island nearby. The old cemetery (no longer in use) is set back from the sea and holds many of the original pioneers. The trail from the beach is choked with salal and many of the headstones have toppled, their inscriptions faint or indistinguishable. Alma's six brothers and many of her friends have preceded her. It is a time of waiting.

Often, on a damp winter day, Alma and I will visit in the kitchen, made cosy by her ancient wood-burning stove. Pictures of her extended family surround her, and Johanna's Fabrik-Marke sewing machine sits in a place of honor in the parlour. Occasionally, on a suddenly-warm spring day (days that arrive on the west coast long before the rest of Canada breaks hibernation) we will seek the sun. We get into the car and point its nose south, toward Long Beach, site of Johanna and Jacob's original homestead.

The former trail to Grice Bay has long ago been reclaimed by the rainforest and so we take the newer road, the one that leads to the boat ramp. We pass the golf course, where Canada geese compete with humans for the greens, and a long ball could conceivably land on an airport runway. Alma knows just where the first Trumpeter swans of the season should be and so we park the car opposite a small peninsula/island—depending on the tide, and wait. We aren't disappointed, and we sit comfortably, observing the beautiful birds through the binoculars.

Across the bay, with natural deterioration and eventual disappearance of man-made structures, the quiet scene appears much as it did when Jacob brought Johanna there as a bride. The mud flats backgrounded by mountains, an eagle wheeling overhead in the updrafts, and over all a sense of calm. Alma grows quiet and I sense that she is seeing it as it must have been during her childhood. When the shadows of the late afternoon begin to lengthen, we turn for home.

FIVE

Children of the Lights

Although the family would later experience tragedy
within its rocky environs, in the beginning the island was a place
of enchantment for the children. They roamed as diminutive
nomads amongst its trees and bushes, gullies and rock faces. Olive
remembers her favourite place was a tiny, child-sized crescent of
coarse white sand on the windward side of the island, which the
children quickly christened "Shell Beach." With every tide an
infinite variety of shells was deposited upon its shores in every
colour and shape imaginable: large white moon snails, dusky pink
scallops, grey sand dollars and amber whelks, their living organ-
isms long since extracted by more predatory species. It was a mar-
vellous display which changed daily.

The children never tired of gathering the shells and laying them on top of logs to bleach in the sun, then adding the more
exotic varieties to their steadily growing collection. Little Enid
could usually be found exploring one of the intertidal pools that
ringed the island at low tide. These small basins teemed with life,

and were irresistible to a child: sea palms, many-spined purple sea urchins, brilliantly coloured anemones (the flowers of the sea), crabs and small fish, red sponge and vari-coloured starfish, some luminous, winking with inner light. The variety of sea life, seen and experienced on the island's shores—and beyond—was endless, and the children never grew tired of exploring their island world.

The year was 1904 and the Lennard Island lightstation—most up to date on the continent—was newly constructed, to give much needed assistance to the many trading vessels that plied the stormy shipping lanes of the west coast, an area of treacherous seas and unforgiving reefs. Frank, the children's father, had been part of the crew that erected the sturdy tower and residence on the small windswept island off the coast of Tofino. He had applied and been accepted for the position of lighthouse keeper, for the princely sum of ninety dollars per month.

Frank, his wife Annie, and their six children—Lilly fifteen, Burdett fourteen, Ethel twelve, Noel ten, Olive seven, and Enid four—travelled up the coast from Port Alberni (then known simply as Alberni) aboard the Canadian Pacific supply boat *Queen City* to Clayoquot where they stayed overnight. The next morning the family was transported to the island by launch, their belongings towed behind on a scow. At that point their worldly possessions included: one cow with calf, one dog and three cats, a sewing machine and three sea chests filled with bolts of material and remnants of Annie's trousseau.

As they entered the gap between the reefs below the landing area, Lilly noticed the amber bulbs of kelp floating in the channel and remarked upon the large number of "onions" that had been spilled into the water.

The first weeks were spent in a small supply cabin until their new home was finished. So began their years on the lights, years that even today, eighty-five years later, are etched indelibly upon the minds of the former children.

The children came of British stock, their grandfather and great-grandfather having served in India as officers in the East India Army. Frank's father contracted "jungle fever" and returned to his home in Eastbourne, England, where he taught at a college and later married and had twelve children. In 1875 the couple booked passage aboard the *Circassian* for Quebec City, with a view to emigrating to Canada. It was during this voyage that twelve year old Frank began a journal—a habit he would adhere to during much of his lifetime and one that gave a fascinating glimpse into the sights and mores of the time.

As the ship entered the Gulf of St Lawrence, he wrote of the clearing of miles of virgin timberland along both sides of the river bank, from Rimousky to Levis, and the large rafts topped by small houses, quarters for the river crew. The long streams of acrid smoke threatened to obscure the horizon and the journey was slow. The family was delighted by the picturesque Thousand Islands, viewed from the deck. They visited the Plains of Abraham and Niagara Falls where they walked over the newly constructed extension bridge. Eventually Frank's parents decided to return to England but the young boy could not forget the country whose vastness was only hinted at by the burgeoning eastern settlements.

At the age of sixteen, Frank signed on as an apprenticed seaman aboard the barque *Renown* and sailed from London, bound for Melbourne, Australia. Thus began ten years of "shipping before the mast"—years that would take him seven times around the Horn and six times around the world. In the southern waters of the Caribbean, to break the monotony, the men would swim behind the ship, keeping a sharp lookout for sharks. They augmented their fresh food supply by harpooning porpoises and trapping the ever present albatross. By law, rations of fresh lime juice were dispensed daily to members of the crew (to ward off scurvy), along with the traditional tot of rum. Frank wrote of the picturesque windmills lining the shores of Barbados, the energy harvested being used to power their sugar mills. He eventually contracted malaria while the boat was berthed at St. Kitts and returned to England to regain his health.

He had been corresponding with a beautiful young woman he had met, through a shipmate, on one of his former shore leaves and it was at this time that Frank and Annie decided to not be parted again. They were married quietly at Wandsworth in December 1889 and left almost immediately aboard the *Sardinian* for a new life in Canada. The voyage across the North Atlantic in mid-winter was an ordeal and Annie spent much of the time in her bunk, violently seasick. Upon disembarking in Halifax the couple boarded the train for the west. At that time there were stoves in each railway car, to be used for heating and cooking, and the trip across the ice-bound countryside was passed in relative comfort.

In Vancouver they saw the original wooden buildings lining the waterfront (although many had been destroyed in the disastrous fire of 1886), and wooden sidewalks built atop stumps. They took the *Princess Louise,* a side-wheeler night ferry, for Victoria where, to their surprise, they saw much evidence of chain gangs. Finally, they boarded the E&N railway (built by the coal baron Dunsmuir) for Comox, where they bought two acres preparatory to erecting their first Canadian home. At that time much of the west coast lay under five feet of snow and it wasn't until spring that Frank and Annie were able to clear their land and begin building. By then Annie was expecting the couple's first child.

Over the next several years Frank worked at various jobs: carpenter, mate aboard a coal ship that supplied the Gulf Islands, and telegraph linesman with the crew that laid the original line to the outer west coast. Most jobs took him away from home for long periods of time and, when the job of lighthouse keeper on Lennard Island became available, both Annie and Frank agreed it was a welcome opportunity. There were many ends to tie up before they moved to the isolated outpost and they both set about preparing themselves in every way for the rather drastic change in lifestyle. Annie had been having problems with her teeth, and, fearing complications during their time on the island, she visited a dentist and had all of them extracted—without benefit of anaesthetic!

And so the couple, with their six children, became an integral part of Her Majesty's maritime service, an experience that would test their loyalties and inner resources to the limits. It was the first day of November, 1904 when Lennard Light began flashing its beam across the cold seas of the Pacific and even though the island lay a distance of only three miles from the settlement at Clayoquot, it might well have been three hundred miles once the winter storms began. The first Christmas was spent observing the awesome forces of nature as a gale struck the area, with winds of hurricane force. The crew that had worked to install the fog-station was marooned on the island and spent the holiday with the family. Olive remembers they played word games and made popcorn, and the men taught the children songs.

Between winter storms, Frank and oldest son Burdett were able to get out in their rowboat and keep the family supplied with fresh fish and other delicacies of the sea. Once a month the supply ship *Quadra* called, an event eagerly looked forward to by parents and children alike. On that morning they would all work together, unloading the goods and carefully storing them away. That evening the family would sit down to a sumptuous meal, the star attraction being a roast of beef or occasionally pork.

It wasn't until spring that the family was able to begin to till the scanty soil and plant a garden. Most of the trees on the island had been felled due to a misunderstanding about where the buildings were to stand and, as a result, the tender garden shoots were ever at the mercy of the cutting winds and torrential rains. Nevertheless, the garden produced an amazing variety of fresh vegetables, and even some fruit. The family made the island uniquely their own. Eventually they had a herd of goats, seventeen cats, dogs, and flocks of chicken and geese.

Coloma

That first year, Frank managed to continue the children's education with the help of text books they had brought to the island. During the second year it was learned that if a sufficient number of children could be found in the area a school could be opened in Tofino and a certified teacher employed. After much soul searching, Annie and Frank decided that the children from Lennard Light would be allowed to swell the ranks of students. (It is remembered by former students that few teachers stayed longer than one year in the isolated little settlement, some left before their year was up.)

Each Monday morning the older children would cast off from the rocks below the house, together with their favourite cats, and row across Templar Channel, around the point and into the dock below the promontory. They would tie up the boat and make their way to the schoolhouse a short distance away. The parents, watching from the shore as they left, never knew if they had arrived safely until they saw them returning across the channel on Friday afternoon, weather permitting. Often Frank would meet them half-way in the lighthouse boat.

During the week the children lived in a sturdy two-story house that Frank had built, toward the day when the family might wish to relocate to the village. They cooked for themselves, kept the house tidy, made good marks in school, and still managed time for play, essential to any child's life. The adults of the village, (many of them friends of Annie and Frank) took a benevolent interest in the well-being of these lighthouse children and, while not making it obvious, kept a close eye on the youngsters.

It was during one of the Friday afternoon crossings that the children narrowly escaped disaster. Halfway across the strait one of the oarlocks broke and the young mariners attempted to set the sail they had aboard. During the procedure, an errant wave capsized the canoe, tossing the children (and their beloved cats) into the frigid sea. Fortunately, Frank and Burdett were meeting them that day, observed the accident, and rowed with all possible haste to the spot, half a mile distant. Ethel and Noel were holding onto the overturned craft and supporting little Olive, who couldn't swim. To Noel's disgust, one cat clung tenaciously to the top of his head, claws firmly embedded in his scalp. The second was found in the airspace beneath the canoe and the third drifted away, out of sight. The children were quickly hauled into the larger boat and taken home to Annie's tender ministrations. Burdett righted the canoe and rowed it home.

Frank later wrote of the terrifying incident: "For some days I had the vision before my eyes, of the upturned canoe & the splashing in the water, as I saw it at first. I may say here that we cut the canoe in half & used it for a feed bin after that, as it was a cranky canoe & not fitted for those waters & I did not want any more accidents with it. I was thankful Annie had not been in our boat when this occurred as she is expecting another addition to the family." Thereafter, the children made the hazardous trip in a rowboat towed by a larger launch.

In the early morning hours of Boxing Day, 1906—a year that saw a succession of early winter gales rake the shipping lanes—Frank spied a derelict vessel from the windows of the light tower. She was the barque *Coloma,* wrecked on the rocks off Cape Beale, far to the south, drifting toward Wickaninnish Island, topmasts gone, torn signal flag drooping from the lower mast. Frank raced to launch a boat to go to assist the craft, not knowing whether any of the crew had survived. Seventeen year old Ethel accompanied him. Their selfless actions were subsequently related to readers of the *Montreal Herald* several days later, with Ethel being compared to a heroine of the English lighthouses.

> "*Vancouver Island's west coast has developed a twentieth century Grace Darling, and she is the 17 year old daughter of the Dominion lightkeeper at Lennard Island, Clayoquot Sound. Through the circumstances that her heroism was unmarked by spectacular salvation of life and through her own modesty, her brave deed has until now been unrecorded. ...(The barque*

*Coloma) after her distressed company had been taken off by the
Government steamer Quadra, was abandoned and drifted
northward where it was sighted one mile north of the lightstation. There was a high sea and heavy surf running, but
Lightkeeper F. C. Garrard and his daughter, the sole inmates of
the lonely watchtower, believing that lives were at stake, did not
hesitate and while they were getting out their boat, the Coloma
struck on the reefs. They pulled their way inch by inch thither,
only to find no sign of life, and the vessel broken in two by
impact with the reef, the after part only being above water.
Garrard and his daughter returned to the lighthouse exhausted
and heavy hearted, believing that the Coloma's crew had per-
ished. It was not until several days later that they learned of the
rescue through Mrs. Patterson's intrepidity and the promptness
of the Quadra.*

Both Frank and Ethel were modest in their accounts of
the incident, deferring instead to the valourous Mrs Patterson,
wife of the keeper at Cape Beale, who, at the height of the storm,
trekked through the rainforest, at times wading in icy water up to
her waist, to get help for the beleaguered ship and its crew. The
aftermath of these events greatly weakened her health, contribut-
ing to her death five years later from tuberculosis.

Annie found the years on Lennard difficult. She began to
experience recurring bouts of depression. Frank felt much of the
problem was due to loneliness and he made a point of bringing
friends to the island whenever possible. One of the most frequent
visitors was the wife of the postmaster at Clayoquot and the two
became warm friends. One year, for Annie's birthday, Frank gave
her one of the first phonographs (Edison) in the area, which enabled
the family to enjoy the music of the times—most notably the spirited renditions of Harry Lauder. However, Annie became increasingly worried about the inherent dangers present in their daily lives,
most notably the trips the children made to school. As well as the
school crossings, Ethel had nearly drowned on one of the trips into

town with her father and Annie herself had a nasty experience when her skirt caught in the flywheel of their new gas-engined boat while she was holding the youngest child.

The arrival of baby Edward, in November, 1906, seemed to dispel some of Annie's melancholy and indeed, the child, coming to the couple in middle life, became the centre of the family. "He grew up full of life & vigor and never seemed to be ill in any way. He seemed to be, as he grew older and could run about, not only unusually active, but very seldom cried even under what might well be provocation." The toddler delighted in following his sisters and brothers on their daily explorations.

In January of 1908, Frank was notified of an upcoming inspection of the station and in preparation for the arrival of the official aboard the supply ship, Annie and Frank launched a marathon cleaning bee both within the tower and the house. Floors and walls were scrubbed, windows were washed and shined, machinery oiled and polished, even the grounds were tidied and raked. During a break, Burdett sat at the table with his fourteen month old brother over his shoulder. The child spied fragments of crystals on the shelf behind, fallen unnoticed from a closed tin, and quickly scooped them into his mouth, no doubt thinking they were sugar.

No one witnessed the incident but soon the baby began to scream in agony and it wasn't until Annie discovered alkali burns on the little fingers that the family realized that Edward had swallowed lye. Noel ran to the tower, screaming for his father and Frank administered a little sweet oil causing the baby to vomit blood. Although the seas were exceedingly rough that day, they immediately launched a boat and made their way to the temporary hospital at Clayoquot. The doctor once again induced vomiting and the child seemed easier, finally falling into an exhausted sleep. The parents remained at Clayoquot for several days, during which time Edward improved to the point where they finally took him home. A few days later, however, the baby had a relapse and died, in spite of all possible efforts to revive him.

The family was devastated. Frank and Burdett fashioned a tiny coffin for the baby and they all made the sad trip to the village where services were held. Then one final trip over the water to Morpheus Island, where Edward was interred in the little cemetery on the edge of the sea. After the funeral, Frank and Annie returned to Lennard together. Friends felt Annie should perhaps stay on at the house in Tofino with the children for a while, rather than return to the scene of the tragedy, but the couple couldn't bear to be parted during this time of sadness. The entire family mourned their loss and grew closer.

Despite Lennard being the "most modern of stations," it was necessary for either Frank or the assistant keeper to spend nights in the tower as the clock required winding every 2 1/2 hours. After the loss of baby Edward, Enid would often carry her blankets out to the tower and spend the night curled up near her father, an arrangement that brought comfort to both of them.

Annie made a valiant attempt to take up her life on the lightstation again but the memories were too painful. Visions of little Edward arose wherever she turned on the island. Despite Frank's patience and understanding her depression returned, deeper than ever, and it became obvious that the family must leave the lightstation. Finally Frank tendered his resignation and made plans to pre-empt land on Vargas Island nearby. Late in the summer his replacement arrived, and the family loaded their belongings onto a small scow and left Lennard Island for the last time.

Vargas, named in 1792 for a Spanish Governor, had white sand beaches, protected coves and a deep water channel, and for these reasons was thought to be a logical place for development. Along with other settlers, most of them English, Frank and Annie built a home on Vargas and planned to farm their land. Annie seemed to receive a new lease on life in the new location, surrounded by friends. Just before Christmas of that turbulent year Annie gave birth to a girl, christened Evelyn. However, Vargas became a bitter disappointment to the homesteaders as its damp marshy soil proved unsuitable for farming, and when war broke out in Europe, most people left, never to return. Annie and Frank eventually gave up island living for their home in Tofino where Frank became chief telegraph operator and linesman, and the couple had many happy years there surrounded by family. Annie died in Olive's arms in 1936 at the age of sixty-nine and Frank followed her seven years later. Both lie buried on Morpheus Island along with Edward.

The children of Lennard Light took various paths in life although most never lived far from the sound of a fog horn. When war broke out in Europe in 1914, Burdett enlisted in the army and served overseas where he contracted tuberculosis. He was invalided home to a sanitorium in the interior of British Columbia and died there at the age of thirty, several months after marrying his childhood sweetheart. Noel served in both World Wars but most of his life was spent in Port Alberni working as an Indian agent and boat builder. Lilly became a nurse, and served with distinction in a large military hospital in England during both wars. She never married, and spent the latter years of her life in California. The other girls worked either as telephone or telegraph operators in Tofino and later Port Alberni. They married men involved in the forestry industry.

Today Enid and Olive are the sole survivors of the original lighthouse family. The two sisters, both widows, live together in a comfortable apartment in the James Bay area of Victoria, not far from the harbour where Frank and Annie disembarked so many years ago to begin their married life. Both take an avid interest in the activities of their families and friends and experience a particular enjoyment when the conversation turns to the west coast of yesteryear.

SIX

You Go Find Gold?

Gold! The precious metal was discovered in the Bedwell River in 1865 by a member of an English botanical expedition and, while the coastal mountains have not (to this date), yielded a spectacular amount, in earlier years their treasures, which also included copper and quartz, formed the basis of a promising, if not always reliable mining industry. The Bedwell River has its source high in the mountains of the interior that form the rugged spine of Vancouver Island and it drains into Bedwell Sound, one of the three principle arms that encircle Clayoquot Sound. As soon as word of the discovery of gold reached the larger centres the race was on.

Prospectors, hampered by snow-choked valleys in the winter and rushing, unnavigable streams in the rainy season, and also the absence of roads into the area, sent their ore samples and the occasional gold nugget south by boat to the Mining Recorder's office in Clayoquot and later to Tofino. The Bedwell attracted fledgling prospectors, entrepreneurs and speculators, lured by

65

visions of rich claims, a steady income or the gamble of a lifetime. At one time a small cluster of wooden shacks near the head of the river (grandiosely named Bear City by Chinese placer miners, the early settlers of the area), offered the bare essentials of life to those men determined to make their fortunes in this, one of the forerunners of the fabulously rich strike in the Klondike, far to the north. A few of these individualists brought their families, fewer still met and married, one of the young local ladies, and the descendants of these early pioneers of the west coast, be they harvesters of the mountains, sea, or forest, form the core of many a coastal community today.

One of those who heard of the opportunities available on the west coast of the island was a young husband and father in Vancouver. After consulting with his wife, he began building a sturdy thirty-six foot wooden boat from cedar trees that crowded their property and obtained a contract to haul supplies to the mining camp at the head of the Bedwell. Next the couple sold their property in Point Grey, today the prestigious site of the University of British Columbia, and at dawn, on a crisp day in the fall of 1921, set sail from Coal Harbour on Vancouver's waterfront, headed for the wilds of Clayoquot Sound.

Their daughter Arline was five at the time and still vividly remembers the trip. Neither Arline, her mother, nor her grandmother, who accompanied the little family, had ever experienced an ocean voyage in a small boat and the vessel had barely cleared Prospect Point before all three were miserably seasick. Later that day, soon after they entered the Strait of Juan de Fuca, off the coast of Victoria, a sudden storm struck, with vicious winds and mountainous waves. The boat began to founder and take on water, until finally the engine stopped. Arline's father detached the small dinghy and endeavored to tow the larger boat away from the rocks. By now it was dark and with the storm increasing in intensity, the rescue attempt was doomed to failure. The family abandoned the boat and were able to make their way through the surf and over the rocks to the shore where they stood huddled together in the freezing rain, watching as the gallant little vessel, *Raincoast Spirit,* was rhythmically pounded to bits against the rocks.

Suddenly Arline's father became aware of a light flashing in the distance and, after reassuring his family, began to walk toward it. It turned out to be the Trial Island lighthouse. This lightstation was constructed in 1906 upon a barren rock shelf situated in treacherous Enterprise Channel off the coast of Victoria. The lighthouse keeper and his wife were used to having unexpected guests thrown up on their shores and shortly thereafter, the family was enjoying dry clothes and hot food, while the terror of the night receded. They were forced to stay on Trial Island for ten days, until the steamship *Princess Maquinna* made its next regular run up the coast.

They arrived in Tofino late at night and were able to hire someone to ferry them over to Stone Island which they had rented. The island was owned by a former missionary and there was an old house that went with the property but it hadn't been lived in for several years. While Arline's father set about lighting the lamps and making a fire, the women busied themselves making up beds and settling the family for the night. Arline remembers her mother moving some shingles stored in the bedroom only to find several lizards scurrying away.

During those early years Arline's father was away for much of the time. He leased a boat, taking freight up the Bedwell River, then transporting it overland by packhorse to the mining camp, a distance of thirteen miles. Arline's mother, raised in the city, faced most of the challenges of that first winter on her own, with the help of her mother. The winter of 1921-22 was cold, with more snow than usual. For the first time in living memory some of the smaller coves were covered with ice. Often during those first months, after a particularly heavy fall of snow, the women were forced to climb to the rooftop to shovel off the accumulated drifts, lest the roof collapse.

At one point that first winter they were completely out of firewood, and the situation was serious for the women and small child, as Arline's father had been delayed at the Bedwell by heavy snows that choked the mountain passes. Finally one evening came when they were forced, for the first time since their arrival, to eat a cold supper and go to bed between clammy sheets. During the night there was a fierce storm and, when they awoke in the morning, they found driftwood of all sizes piled high on the beach below, as if in answer to their prayers. Often they were kept awake by the barking of sea lions hauled out on the rocks below. In March, Arline's grandmother returned to her well-ordered life in Vancouver, declaring she didn't know why anyone would choose to live in such a God-forsaken place.

Fortunately, with the coming of spring, life on the island began to improve. There was a small orchard, with plum trees and apples, and many different types of berries, which were gathered and preserved for the months ahead. At low tide they harvested clams from the beaches and waded out knee deep to rake in large Dungeness crabs which lay concealed beneath the eel grass. Fish, ducks, and geese were plentiful and occasionally the family feasted on venison. They planted a large vegetable garden and rowed the short distance to Clayoquot to purchase their staples in the general store.

Often at night the eery sound of chanting would reverberate through the inky darkness as the Indians held their pow-wows in the village of Opitsaht on neighbouring Meares Island. Sometimes the natives would come in their war canoes to the beach below the house, wrapped in blankets and wearing distinctive cedar-bark hats. Remaining seated in their canoes, they would pound their paddles against the wooden sides, a sound guaranteed to strike fear into the hearts of all within hearing distance. Arline's mother would hurry down to the beach to trade freshly baked bread for fish : "Who would refuse them?" Later, as the Indians grew to know them they gave the family gifts of ladies' bags and jewellery boxes, beautifully woven from cedar bark.

68

The most exciting event in the lives of the early west coasters, and one that brought them together for a day of socializing, was the regular arrival of the popular ship *Princess Maquinna*. In this age of instant communication, shopping malls, and fast food outlets it may require some imagination to appreciate the importance of the regular visits of this supply vessel. Named for the daughter of Chief Maquinna of the Nootka Indian tribe, the one-funnelled, single-screw ship was built in Esquimalt and launched in 1913. The ship could accommodate four hundred day passengers and had one hundred berths. She was berthed in the inner harbour of Victoria where, promptly at 11:00 P.M. every tenth day, she slipped her lines and began her northern run of twenty-six scheduled stops, bringing the necessities of life to those in mining camps, canneries, and small coastal communities.

To sail aboard the *Maquinna* was to experience the charm and ambience of steamship travel of a by-gone era. Many immigrants bound for mine, pre-emption, or marital bed, had their first glimpse of their new home from the polished decks of this supply ship. The ship and its genial captain and helpful crew came to occupy a special place in west coast hearts. The captain was once heard to explain to a curious passenger his success in navigating this, the most dangerous of coasts: "I don't know so much where the rocks are, I just know where they aren't." Occasionally he was called upon to rescue survivors of a maritime disaster or deliver a baby. For some passengers the delicious meals, comfortable beds, and camaraderie experienced with the crew and fellow passengers would be their last taste of gracious living for a long time.

On boat day, people stopped whatever they were doing, freshened up, and headed for the village. Once there, they visited with friends and neighbours, picked up their mail and supplies and left their orders for the next trip. As one old timer put it succinctly, "You received EVERYTHING on the *Maquinna*. If you hadn't remembered to order something—especially your booze—you checked the manifest to see who had!"

The gallant ship, last of a series of west coast supply ships was retired from the Canadian Pacific Steamship Lines in 1952 and served out the remainder of her days as an ore carrier.

After five years Arline's parents bought nearby Neilson Island for five hundred dollars. They cleared the land, built a house, and put in a large garden. By then Arline's younger brother had arrived and in good weather the children rowed over to attend school in Tofino. During the winter they supplemented their studies by taking correspondence courses.

Several years later Arline's father began a pile driving business and, being the oldest child, she was expected to work alongside him. She accepted that life, as she loved the outdoors. The only drawback was her fear of heights. At times she would have to fight dizziness and nausea as her father lashed his young daughter into a sling and pulled her to the top of a tall tree to thread a cable through a block. They worked hard, but they also had their good times.

One of her favourite memories is of the quiet evening she and her father went fishing in the channel separating their island from the peninsula and she managed to reel in a twenty-five pound salmon. Her mother cut off thick steaks, fried them in fresh butter and served them with freshly baked bread. Arline can still remember the taste of that fish in her mouth. She spent her twenty-first birthday on Lennard Light cooking for the crew that was building the new power plant.

The main entertainment during those years was the Saturday night dances, held in the Tofino community hall. Arline began going when she was thirteen. "We broke our necks to get there, no matter how far we had to row." Entire families would come. The women brought food for the midnight suppers and, as the evening progressed, the younger children were settled for sleep on the benches. Many a future relationship had its inception at the community dance. People from the surrounding islands stayed until morning and crossed the water at first light—weather permitting.

Arline met her husband-to-be at one of the dances. Sam was a young prospector from Victoria, and somewhat of a local celebrity because he had just hiked over the mountains from Port Alberni. In those days a young man could purchase a miner's certificate for five dollars and, armed with this, and the most basic of equipment, he was free to join other fledgling miners in their pursuit of that one big strike. His degree of success was limited only by his knowledge of geology, stamina, patience, and in some cases, just sheer luck. For all of the aforementioned reasons, Sam became one of the best. Arline admits it wasn't love at first sight but Sam was persistent and they were married five years later.

By then war in Europe had been declared and the next few years were busy. Sam was often away for weeks at a time prospecting for minerals needed in Canada's war effort while Arline was at home with the chidren. In 1939 they were living in a floathouse moored in Cowichan Bay. By this time they had two toddlers and Arline lived in fear that someday one of the children might fall into the water and drown, despite the fact that Sam had built a fence around the barge. She finally told Sam, when he returned from one of his prospecting trips, that they must move onto land. They located a beautiful little home in the nearby village. "It was like a doll house, with antique furniture, hand-painted plates hanging in the kitchen, and lovely gardens." The owners were stranded in England due to the outbreak of war and required someone to rent their property until they could return. The rent was twenty-five dollars a month. And so, Sam and Arline sold the floathouse and moved to the village.

One of their tasks during the move was to inform their Chinese vegetable man, who called weekly, that they were leaving. This gentleman, a tall Manchurian, had come to know the family and enjoyed playing with the tow-headed children. He knew Sam was a prospector and immediately enquired, "You go find gold?" Sam replied that, while he always enjoyed discovering gold, it was usually his fate to uncover baser metals. About a month later, (by

Cowichan Lake 1939

now firmly established in their new home) Sam went to answer a knock at the door. There stood their friendly vegetable man. Both men looked at each other in surprise. At a glance, the Manchurian took in their improved circumstances and then enquired, in tones of astonishment, tinged with awe, "You find gold—AL-LEADY?"

The family continued to move often as they followed Sam on his explorations. It was an interesting life, and they saw some beautiful country, but as the babies continued to arrive, Arline eventually grew tired of constantly moving and of having few conveniences. Finally she suggested to Sam that they go home—to Tofino. They bought six acres in town, in partnership with Arline's parents. The area, then known as Uzatses Point, was the site of an ancient Indian midden.

In earlier days local tribes would leave their principle villages to follow the seasonal movements of fish, game birds and wildlife. They would load their large canoes with supplies and travel to various protected bays. While the men fished, intercepting the spawning herring and various types of salmon, the women would gather sea gull eggs, clams, and cedar bark. Large racks were built to dry the fish which would serve as their main source of food over the coming months. The midden on Uzatses Point has yielded many artifacts, including a well preserved skeleton.

Although prospecting would always be Sam's first love, once settled in Tofino he went into the logging business, forming a partnership with his father-in-law. They located a deep-water cove in Ucluelet in which to dump their logs, which Sam located by beachcombing. This was a traditional way of logging—before the advent of modern harvesting techniques—and a good way to begin in the business.

Sam would patrol the waters in a small boat, scanning the beaches for stray logs that had broken away from large booms. When he had several, he would then tow them down to the holding pen in Ucluelet and sell them. The large logging companies left much waste behind, even then. In spite of this, a person had to pay dearly for a small "show", an area in which he could log.

Eventually Sam bought a helicopter, "How he loved that thing." It permitted him to scan the beaches for logs and the tops of mountains for minerals. It also allowed him to clear the creeks of debris and logs without harming the precious fish spawn.

Today the couple continue to live on their original property. Much of the region that Sam used to prospect is now contained within Strathcona Park and has become an area of contention between environmentalists and those who would mine. Sam and Arline are of the generation of west coasters that took pride in making their living from the treasures of the area in which they chose to settle and raise their family. A different shade of pride perhaps from the modern day workers whose professional ethics and projected yields are formulated by multinational companies and governments whose goals have become highly suspect.

From the windows of the couple's home can be seen Neilson Island and the mountains that Sam came to know so intimately. Arline spends much of her time cultivating her garden and occasionally turns over an arrowhead or other traces of earlier days. Some of their children live close by and Arline and Sam recently became great-grandparents for the first time.

SEVEN

Dark Cloud: Fairest Day

Frances and Isabel are cousins and each grew to young woman-hood on the west coast, in the never-again-to-be-so-innocent days preceding World War II, the bombing of Pearl Harbour, and the displacement of Japanese Canadians to remote inland areas of Canada.

Isabel was born in Steveston and moved as a child to Tofino. Her father was a fisherman and the family settled at Eik Bay, which in those days was a short distance from the village, a tranquil little cove with rich mud flats and site of a former Indian midden. Growing up in the quiet fishing village, she remembers an idyllic childhood. She attended school in a one-room schoolhouse, along with the white children of the area, many of European immigrant parentage. One of her closest friends was a little Norwegian girl, daughter of one of the founding families of Tofino.

One of Isabel's fondest memories is of accompanying Christine home after school and sitting around the large kitchen table while Christine's mother plied them both with freshly baked buns and glass after glass of sweet milk—both of which were a novelty in the young Japanese girl's life. Within the Japanese community, age-old traditions were maintained. Isabel still treasures a sepia-toned picture from that time showing herself and five little classmates, beguilingly dressed in kimonos and obiis, their feet shod in getas. They are twirling waxed paper parasols and each has a mischievous twinkle in her eye.

When Isabel was eleven, a family crisis threatened to alter her life forever. It was customary in those days for the fishing fleet to return to the harbour each evening. One night, to the consternation of the family, Isabel's father did not return. At dawn the next morning her uncle went looking for him and found the boat drifting aimlessly, far out to sea. Isabel's father, alone on the boat, had suffered a stroke the previous afternoon and lay helpless in the cabin. His boat was towed home and the family sent for Mrs. Igarachi. There was no hospital in Tofino at that time and Mrs. Igarachi served the Japanese people not only as nurse and midwife, but often as doctor as well. She was held in high esteem by everyone in the village. She explained to the family that the father had suffered a stroke, told them how to nurse him, and left directions for special exercises.

A year later, in 1935, when he could finally walk again, he left for Japan to visit family and friends. In 1936 he sent for his wife and children. Isabel and her mother joined him on the main island of Honshu, while her two older brothers chose to remain in Tofino. Isabel attended school in Japan and enjoyed life there, although her heart remained on the Canadian west coast. Finally, in 1940, at the age of nineteen, she sailed for Canada, accompanied by an aunt, aboard the Japanese passenger ship *Heian-Maru,* a voyage lasting fifteen days. The young woman was bound for Tofino and an arranged marriage, negotiated by an uncle. In

November of that year, Isabel married Robert, a young Japanese fisherman who had recently purchased his first fishing boat.

Isabel's cousin Frances was born in Vancouver and her family moved to Tofino when she was still a baby. They lived at Storm Bay (today Cox Bay) on the outer coast, now one of the prime destination points for tourists. There were eight Japanese families in the tiny settlement and all the men were fishermen. Her father died when Frances was five and the family was forced to move back to Vancouver so that her mother could find employment. Her oldest brother left school after he completed grade ten and the family was able, by pooling resources, to help him buy an uncle's fishing licence. Because of the strict quota system, a commercial fishing licence was, and still is, very expensive. It is often passed down through a family as a birthright, a valuable possession. The family moved back to Tofino and life went on in the most pleasant and structured of ways.

One of Frances' most vivid childhood memories is of her first Canadian ice cream cone, consumed on the beach during Clayoquot Days while sitting with her mother, listening to the band from Christie School play "Bicycle Built for Two." As a widow, her mother was hard pressed to provide for five children. One of her business ventures was to make tofu, which the siblings took turns delivering to the Japanese families of the area. Frances still remembers a white girl, two years older than she, who used to waylay her on her way home from making deliveries and snatch the proceeds of her sales. (The same juvenile bully also purloined the small girl's Sunday school collection coin whenever possible.)

Apart from the obligatory childhood crises, common the world over, Frances too recalls a happy childhood: one lived in harmony with nature and neighbours. Even the outbreak of war in Europe did not seem to pose any serious threat to west coast Canadian citizens. Frances became engaged to Ken, yet another Japanese fisherman, in the summer of 1941.

Then came the bombing of Pearl Harbour by Japan on December 7th., 1941. In the ensuing tumult, paranoia swept the vulnerable west coast. Even in the face of this, Frances and Ken decided to go ahead and marry: after all, they had been born in this country and knew themselves to be loyal Canadian citizens. Shortly thereafter, all Japanese fishermen were required to surrender their fishing boats to the Canadian government. They were allowed to sail their own boats, with a Canadian sailor aboard, to the slough in New Westminster. Once there, the boats were auctioned off at bargain prices, with the former owners receiving a token payment.

One morning in March of 1942, the R.C.M.P. visited each Japanese household on the west coast and told them they must dispose of their belongings immediately and be ready to leave when the *Maquinna* sailed that evening. Each person was allowed to bring one suitcase. Possessions accumulated over a lifetime had to be quickly sorted and packed, or sold, with the essentials being crammed into that one precious suitcase. When the impossibility of meeting such a deadline became clear, the sailing was delayed for a scant twenty-four hours.

Frances remembers her beloved teacher, Miss Katie Hacking, coming to the house just before they left, to give her former student a beautiful white damask table cloth as a wedding gift. The two women hugged, with tears in their eyes. Frances still uses the cloth for very special occasions. Unfortunately such outward manifestations of support from the community were rare.

As the hour of departure drew near, the families began to leave their homes—for many, the only homes they'd ever known—cooking fires still warm, house pets sitting on the doorsteps. They made their way in small groups to the government dock to honor their appointment with destiny, a destiny distressingly beyond their control. Many months later, in January of 1943, the federal cabinet granted an order-in-council which enabled agents of the Canadian government to dispose of Japanese Canadian property without the owners' consent. Frances remembers receiving a cheque for fifty dollars following the sale of their home.

Upon docking in Vancouver, the west coast "aliens," as they were becoming known, were transferred to the exhibition grounds at Hastings Park. They were among the first to be interned and found conditions shockingly primitive. Rather than being housed in the exhibition buildings, they were taken directly to the cattle barns, recently vacated by equine boarders, and each was assigned a horse stall. The animal stench was almost overwhelming. It was still winter and they could see their breath in the air. The husbands were billeted in one building, their wives and children in another. Privacy was next to impossible, although they were eventually given army blankets to hang over the front of the stalls.

That first night, in spite of being exhausted and frightened, few were able to sleep on their bumpy straw mattresses and the silence was punctuated at intervals by children's sharp cries and mothers' scarcely muffled sobs. Fortunately Frances and Isabel were assigned stalls close to one another. Isabel had been breast feeding her first baby, then three months old, but under the stressful conditions her milk dried up, practically overnight.

Hastings Park, and all it implied, still lives in infamy in the minds of all Japanese Canadians interned there. Due to pitifully inadequate hygienic conditions, dysentery quickly broke out, making an already difficult condition even more desperate. Although there was a rudimentary hospital, Mrs. Igarachi was in great demand as the stress and the cold, damp conditions began to take their toll.

The army began to set up bunk beds, which alleviated the overcrowded conditions to a degree, and cooking tents were erected. People lined up outside, no matter what the weather, to receive their rations, ladled onto tin plates. The food was hot and it was nourishing, but it wasn't Japanese. This became a point of contention as time went on. The lucky ones had friends and family in Vancouver who visited and brought traditional foods, knowing full well that their own days of freedom were also numbered. The spacious grounds of Hastings Park became a holding area for hundreds of Japanese-owned vehicles—cars, vans, and trucks. These were eventually auctioned off, with, once again, token payments going to their former owners.

Within a short time, all Canadian-born Japanese men under the age of thirty were given the choice of going to an internment centre or working in a road camp. Many of the young men volunteered to serve in the Canadian Armed Forces in any capacity, but that was not allowed. Both Robert and Ken went to a road camp at Schreiber, Northern Ontario, where they worked hard, although later both said they were treated fairly. They were paid twenty-five cents a day less deductions. Husbands and wives were permitted to write to each other but their letters were censored. Any men who were not Canadian citizens were sent to work camps within British Columbia.

In September of 1942, after seven months at Hastings Park, Frances was relocated to the town of Slocan, in the then-isolated West Kootenay district of interior British Columbia. She and other members of her family endured a tedious, twenty-four hour train trip, sitting upright on stiff woven-wicker seats. She arrived at her new valley home exhausted, wondering what lay ahead.

Located on the shores of historic Slocan Lake, on the floor of the narrow Slocan Valley, the settlement had been one of several flourishing silver mining communities in the area during the 1890s. However, word of even richer strikes in the Klondike lured the miners further north, and by the 1940s the small villages were in danger of becoming ghost towns. The Canadian government was invited by the leaders of these communities to set up the internment camps within their boundaries, in an attempt to revive their failing economies. And so the trains began to arrive in this Swiss-like location, bringing hundreds of confused and resentful displaced citizens of Canada.

In November of that same year, Ken was allowed to leave the road camp in Ontario and join Frances in Slocan. They were assigned a small house, to be shared with another family. It was located in the area known as Popoff's Farm, which fronted onto the lake. Eventually nearly four thousand Japanese Canadians were interned in Slocan. Frances and Ken considered themselves lucky; at least they had a roof over their heads. Many of their friends were forced to spend that first winter living in canvas tents. Unfortunately, the winter of 1942-43 was one of the coldest on record, and the suffering and deprivation of the newly arrived people is something they have never forgotten.

As soon as the weather warmed, the men were put to work constructing new homes. They were encouraged to plant gardens, and the resulting fresh vegetables, always a staple in the Japanese diet, were welcomed. Previously, the only fresh produce available was sold to them by the Doukhobour farmers of the area, who were sympathetic to their plight.

In the beginning, restrictions were strictly enforced. Bans were imposed on travel and passes were required for almost everything, but gradually life improved. Schools were set up, and most of the classes—by choice—began their days by singing "O Canada." Sports teams were organized, the favourite being base-ball, and amateur theatre flourished. The Slocan Community Hospital, previously scheduled to close, became the focus of general medical care during the war years. Frances gave birth to her first two children in Slocan. Life for the internees began to take on a deceptive air of normalcy.

Robert also returned from the road camp at Schreiber and, because they had some savings and were able to declare themselves completely self-supporting, he and Isabel were allowed to settle in Bridge River, north of Vancouver, for the remainder of the war. It was an area of temperate winters and hot, desert-like summers. They too needed permits for all activities, but found them easy to obtain as long as the applicants had a logical reason. They

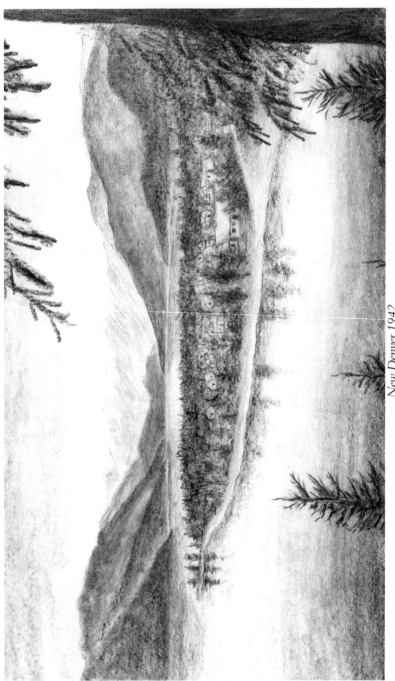

New Denver 1942

were not allowed employment and so occupied themselves by rais-ing fresh vegetables, specializing in tomatoes and pine mushrooms. Isabel gave birth to their second child in Bridge River.

In the closing months of the war, one hundred and fifty volunteers were finally accepted for service with the Canadian Army in the Far East. They worked mainly as interpreters and all served with distinction. On September 2nd. 1945, Japan surren-dered unconditionally, following the destruction of Hiroshima and Nagasaki by atomic bombs dropped by the United States Air Force.

With the cessation of hostilities, Japanese Canadians were given the choice of repatriation to Japan or relocation to Eastern Canada. Frances and Ken moved close to Sudbury where Ken worked at a sawmill. Later he found a job on a mushroom farm near Toronto and the family moved again—to a chicken coop that had been renovated for human occupants. It was during this time that their next two children were born. Isabel and Robert also chose to remain in Canada and moved to Hamilton, where he worked at International Harvester and where they wel-comed the arrival of their third child.

In 1948—for the first time—the Canadian Govern-ment finally extended the franchise to these Canadian citizens of Japanese heritage. The following year, the government of British Columbia followed suit.

Before the war, the Japanese were grudgingly conceded to be the best fishermen on the west coast. They even designed and made their own spoons. Now, in peacetime, the industry wanted them back and the unions were prepared, for the first time, to extend them membership. Officials travelled to Toronto to offer the men contracts and lease them boats. To the dispos-sessed families, many of them unhappy in the unfamiliar environs of the city, it was a welcome opportunity.

Tommy Kimoto, a leader among his people, went ahead and was able to assure his people that, yes, there was indeed a place for the Japanese people on the west coast once again. That place was Ucluelet, sister village to Tofino, and home to some of the friendliest people anywhere.

So it was, that after long years of exile—for most of them, in the land of their birth—the Japanese Canadians began to make their way back to the area that was, in every sense, their home. Many came with mixed feelings of joy and apprehension.

Most of the families settled in Spring Cove, at the entrance to Ucluelet Harbour. It is a place of great natural beauty, once traded by the Indians to an English sea captain for a barrel of molasses. From its shores one can see the fishing fleet heading out to open water and migrating gray whales and hear, in the early morning, the stentorian barking of Steller sea lions hauled out on the rocks below.

Today it is a pleasant and comfortable community, adjacent to bustling Ucluelet, but it was not always so. When Frances and Isabel moved to Spring Cove with their families in the early 1950s there was no road to the village and no electricity. The women pumped water from communal wells and washed clothes down on the beach, among the large rocks. They travelled by boat to the village for supplies. The families faced the hardships and challenges of pioneer living with determination and optimism. After all, they were home.

In the beginning, some of the men preferred to fish their familiar grounds off Tofino and would be away for days at a time. The women were left to cope with life as best they could, and a strong networking system developed. Frances gave birth to six more children in Ucluelet. The children attended school in the village and their parents joined the P.T.A. The settlement slowly grew and gradually the Japanese Canadian people re-entered the mainstream of west coast life.

Many of the women obtained seasonal employment in the fish packing plants, often on the herring roe line. The line is an integral part of many fishing villages, one celebrated in art, prose, and song. Every spring the silvery legions arrive on the west coast in large numbers, returning instinctively to spawn, like the salmon, in the waters of their birth. This bonanza, offered up by the sea, is eagerly awaited—by eagle, seal, and human fisherman. The multitudes are carefully monitored and the harvest strictly controlled. The large seiners with their crews arrive in Ucluelet in advance of the season. The men (and the occasional woman) roam the streets of the village restlessly, knowing the signal to race to the fishing grounds is imminent. A perceptible feeling of tension and anticipation hangs in the air.

Finally the word comes through from the fisheries department who for days have been tracking the fish from the air. The boats are off. The annual herring season may last anywhere from fifteen minutes to two hours and, depending upon the numbers of fish, and the market, can make a fisherman's fortune for the year. Once a boat has its quota, the skipper returns to the harbour and ties up at the packing plant where the herring are sucked from the holds into large containers with amazing speed and noise by hydraulic pumps. Next they are quick frozen for easier handling during processing.

The herring roe line is composed mainly of women, many of them native and Japanese. They stand for long hours on wooden platforms, working with speed, skill, and precision. The women are shod in rubber boots, and are dressed against the cold and arthritis-inducing dampness in long underwear, heavy woollen pants and sweaters, with bright scarves wound around their necks and hair-netted heads. White gowns cover their clothing and these, in turn, are covered by yellow rubber aprons and gloves, which rapidly become spattered with fish-blood and guts.

A conveyor belt delivers the herrings, at a numbing rate, to the women, who quickly, with practiced ease, slit the belly of the tiny fish and "pop" the glistening jewel-like roe into plastic containers. Slit, pop, slit, pop, for hours on end. Sometimes, to break the monotony, the women sing, to the rhythm of their movements. The roe is then airlifted to the lucrative oriental market, where it enhances many a culinary celebration as world class caviar. The eviscerated herrings are bagged as fertilizer for the domestic market. When the season is over, the smell of fish lingers beneath the women's skin for days.

Today, both Isabel and Frances are widows. There are many widows now in Spring Cove. They live in their comfortable homes on the shores of the cove and fill their lives with new interests. Occasionally, Isabel sees Robert's original fishing boat in the area and her thoughts go back to what might have been. Surprisingly, or perhaps not so surprisingly, neither woman confesses to any bitterness. Both are planning a trip back to Bridge River and Slocan soon.

I visited the Slocan Valley, still known locally as the "Silvery Slocan," in May of 1990. I passed signs proclaiming "Kootenays—The Great Escape." In its alpine setting, Slocan lay drowsy in the sun, while the breeze from the lake spawned a blizzard of cherry blossoms which perfumed the air and gathered in pastel drifts along the roadside. Lively Springer Creek, site of many an earlier mining claim, bisects the small village and every street ends at the lumber mill at the edge of the lake.

I look in vain for some trace of those turbulent internment years. Most of the former Japanese homes in the Bay Farm area have disappeared or lie derelict. There are only two Japanese names in the phone book. There are a ball park, tennis courts, loggers' sports area, and a tiny cemetery. One building, on Main Street, houses the essentials of modern life: the Red and White food store, Liquor Store, Sears catalogue office, Video Rentals and Lottery Ticket Centre. The homes are old but well-kept, and the occasional elderly person sits snoozing on a verandah. The only signs of activity on this spring day are the heavily-laden logging trucks that rumble through the sleepy village. This once bustling community has shrunk to little more than one thousand people.

I left Slocan, taking the mountain road, which at this point climbs through the narrow valley, high above the picturesque lake, before dropping once more to the sister village of New Denver, five miles to the north. Close to two thousand Japanese Canadians were interned here, in small, hastily constructed homes, most in the area known as "The Orchard," at the water's edge.

During the war, New Denver was chosen as the site of a new one hundred bed tuberculosis sanitarium, constructed in 1942. A splendid edifice, it sat at the edge of Slocan Lake, its grounds carefully sculptured and tended by the internees, many of whom were former gardeners. They also grew all the fresh fruit and vegetables required for the hospital. The O-Bon Festival, a colourful celebration in remembrance of those who died, was held annually on the manicured lawns, the dancers appearing in traditional costumes.

Both Japanese and Canadian doctors and nurses worked together during this time, in a spirit that transcended the tragic circumstances that brought them together. However, when the Japanese doctor visited patients at the other internment centres, he required a permit and was accompanied by an R.C.M.P. officer. Today there is no trace of the sanitarium except for one building that was moved to the centre of town to serve as a senior citizen's centre.

Later that day, I visited with Mrs. Kamegaya, a Japanese scholar in her mid-eighties, who still teaches the Japanese language to students in the local high school. She lives on a quiet, tree-lined street, and her home, behind a white picket fence, has a serene and welcoming atmosphere. She is surrounded by books, and pictures of former students, who are now scattered throughout the world. As we sat and talked she explained that, of the relatively high number of Japanese residents who continue to live in the valley, most are former patients of the sanitarium and their families.

Mrs. K., as she is known in the village, was born and schooled in Japan. At the age of twenty-two she married a fellow teacher and they came to Canada (New Westminster) to teach Japanese Canadian students. During the war, and their subsequent relocation to New Denver, Mrs. K. continued to teach within the internment centre. When the war was over, the couple chose to remain in Canada. Since her husband's death in 1978 of tubercular-related complications, she has visited Japan on five occasions and each time was troubled by the overcrowded conditions and pollution. Mrs. K. has chosen to live out her days amongst her friends and memories in the beautiful Slocan Valley.

Taking my leave of her, I drove down to the shores of the lake. There, on the site of the former sanitarium, the Japanese residents of the area have begun to create a tranquil memorial garden. I walked along a quiet path and sat on a small bench which faced the water and the Valhalla mountain range beyond. I thought of Frances and Isabel and the last time we had visited. As we sat talking over a cup of tea, Isabel had spoken for both when she summed up their feelings by saying, "I feel it was a very difficult time for everyone and the Japanese Canadian people were caught in the middle. I pray that it could never happen again."

Hanging on the wall, in a place of prominence, was a beautifully framed verse. It was written by a former internee, expressing the reaction of the Japanese Canadians to the redress settlement announced by the Canadian government on September 22nd., 1988.

Our dark cloud of a half century dissipated.
The fairest day
In Japanese-Canadian history
Dawns.
Our joy is unsurpassable.

Takeo Ujo Nakano

Part Two
NOW

EIGHT

The Greening of Meares

The house sat comfortably in a clearing in the forest, almost as if it too grew from the soil. Outside, a truck was parked, its box piled high with colourful fishing floats, and as I made my way down the gravelled path, sea mist rolled in from the ocean, wisps of it seeming to cling to my clothes. Clumps of silver-green sphagnum moss hung from the branches of the large cedar trees that encircled the yard. The scene resembled a stage setting for a play set in the deep south—the invigorating smell of salt air standing in for the perfume of magnolias.

Linda met me at the door, with her four young children close behind. Linda home-schools her children but classes were over for the day and Jesse, twelve, and Ceara, ten, left to play with neighbourhood children, while the toddlers Amber and Adrian contented themselves with a spirited game of tag. Linda and I visited over mugs of steaming herbal tea, sweetened with honey. She mentioned she was tired, having spent most of the night assisting a friend through a home delivery, but spoke glowingly of the experience. A large loom stood in the corner of the living room and colourful skeins of wool of every hue spilled out of a rattan basket on the floor beside it. Bunches of fragrant herbs and strings of onions and garlic hung from the ceiling of the back room.

Linda was born in Haney, a small community outside of Vancouver, and grew up in a rural environment. She and her brothers and sisters had the freedom of the fields, woods, and streams of the area, in the days before the town became a trendy bedroom community of Vancouver and was renamed Maple Ridge. Later in life she attended Dalhousie University in Halifax and travelled throughout Europe and South America, Cuba and Mexico. Next, she lived for several years in the Yukon, where she worked among the native community as a child-care worker.

In the late 1970s Linda moved to Victoria to begin work as a wilderness instructor and counsellor with a government sponsored agency for delinquent children that was fashioned after the highly successful Outward Bound programme. The instructors were assigned to guide young teenagers—most of them from the streets of the inner cities and some in trouble with the law— through a four month wilderness experience. The youngsters, almost without exception, suffered from low self-esteem and lacked confidence. Many had been assigned to the programme against their wishes. The first few days were tough, for student and counsellor alike. But slowly, in spite of themselves, the young people began to trust the instructors and take some small pride in their own accomplishments, whether it be constructing a rope bridge over a swiftly flowing creek or learning to identify and co-exist peaceably among the creatures of the forest. A sense of self-worth began to emerge, one that would serve them well for the remainder of their lives.

It was during these years that Linda met and fell in love with Michael, former Peace Corps worker, shipwright, and long distance solo sailor. They moved to the west coast of the island where they lived aboard Michael's thirty-six foot sailboat *La*

Pincoya (the sea goddess, built in Spain) moored in the Ucluelet harbour. Two years later, when they began a family, they sold the boat and moved to Tofino where they bought a floathouse anchored in Clayoquot Sound on a large wooden barge. Michael found employment as the director of the shipyard at the native village of Opitsaht. The area suited their interests well.

They became interested in, and began to study, various aspects of the aquaculture industry and at length decided to apply for an oyster lease. The science of farming oysters is becoming increasingly precise and the size and quality of oysters harvested in Clayoquot Sound are second to none in the world. The oyster farms of the west coast are now, along with fish farms, the basis of an ever more diverse and lucrative aquaculture, one that continues to grow and support the economy of the area.

After several months of cutting through bureaucratic red tape, Michael and Linda were finally granted an oyster lease. Shortly thereafter they moved the floathouse to the small protected cove aptly named "God's Pocket," within one of Meares Island's sheltering arms. Linda did much of the original seeding of the oyster farm. She worked aboard their herring skiff, a long gondola-shaped aluminum boat and infinitely practical workhorse of the west coast. She constructed a wooden platform at one end where the children played, encased in life jackets at all times. Linda worked at the other end of the boat, stringing the oyster seed onto long lines which were then suspended beneath barrel shaped floats in shallow waters. The water of the cove was constantly changed and energized by the ever nurturing tides.

During their first winter in "God's Pocket," one of the most ferocious storms in recent memory struck the area and the floathouse received a battering. At the height of the storm, one of the large windows blew in, showering the floor with shards of glass and allowing the torrential rains free access, drenching the inside of the home. It was an anxious night for all. The next morning, as Linda and Michael worked to repair the damage, four year old Jesse informed his parents that, should another storm like that strike, he was moving to town. Subsequent winters were spent moored at one of the Tofino wharves or in the lee of Strawberry Island.

Celebrated Meares is the largest island in Clayoquot Sound and is named for the British sea captain who engaged in fur trading along the coast in the 1700s. Ancestral home of Indian tribes for centuries, it holds a special place in west coast hearts. Crowned by Lone Cone, the island is carpeted by a forest of cedar, spruce, Douglas fir and hemlock trees, some of which are one thousand years old and up to fifteen feet in diameter. The island supports many species of wild life. There are small brown island deer, cougars, wolves, and bears. Here the bald eagle reigns supreme, soaring high in the updrafts, and fresh water lakes and streams abound. It is the source of Tofino's drinking water, some of the purest on the face of this tired old earth. Its many small bays yield various species of clams, sea cucumbers and the succulent Dungeness crab. Salmon and dolphin, seal and whale swim in the waters of Clayoquot Sound. The island and its waters have benevolently provided sustenance for the people of the area, native and white alike, for many years.

In the fall of 1979, an incident occurred which set off a chain of events that would change, perhaps forever, the way west coast rainforests and their riches are perceived. A young native woman appeared in the village of Tofino with pictures of clear cut logging that had begun in the Sound by the corporate giant MacMillan Bloedel. It quickly became apparent to many in the area that both their livelihood and lifestyle were threatened. Trees that had stood for centuries would be torn from the earth and hauled away, followed by slash-burning, reducing the once verdant forest to a moonscape and wreaking havoc upon the fragile eco-system of the Sound. The heavy winter rains would wash silt down the mountain sides and into the Sound, unimpeded by any forest.

Not the least consideration was the destruction of some of the most dramatically beautiful scenery on the west coast, basis of a flourishing tourist trade. Concerned citizens decided that some avenue of meaningful dialogue with the logging company must be instituted and that there was no time to lose.

And so it was that the organization "Friends of Clayoquot Sound" was conceived in an artist's studio located in the loft of a former crab cannery overlooking the inlet. The original members, who included Linda and Michael, were people of the area who felt they had a moral responsibility to themselves and succeeding generations to maintain the integrity of the Sound. The Friends researched, and made available to all who wished to learn, documented proof of the possible damage to the region with the loss of yet another prime coastal wilderness area. Next, they petitioned MacMillan Bloedel to present the company's five year logging plan to the people of the area. The company agreed, and an open meeting was held. To the surprise of the company representatives present, a large cross-section of the community attended and actively participated by giving their opinions and requesting further opportunities for input into the process.

As a result of the spirited meeting, the provincial government established the Meares Island planning team, which consisted of representatives of all groups with vested interests in Meares. These included the forest industry, Parks Canada, native people, and the Friends of Clayoquot Sound. The team sat for a full day once a month for four years, which represented a major commitment for the volunteer members. Michael was an eloquent spokesman for the Friends. After four years of meetings, during which little progress was made, MacMillan Bloedel suddenly left and presented their own plan to the government, which in turn drafted an alternate but similar plan. Both were unacceptable to the people of the community, who then presented their own plan to the government. The community plan was completely ignored. It was this callous disregard of time, money, and effort, that finally convinced many people another avenue of protest must be found.

Child in the Garden of Meares

By now word of the Meares Island struggle had spread far beyond the shores of Vancouver Island. People from across Canada and eventually other countries (many of whom had visited the area) began to send support in the form of letters and financial donations. The media became involved. The local people realized that they were being watched on television screens across the nation and redoubled their efforts to present a meaningful protest fully within the confines of the law.

At this time the matter of native land claims became pivotal to the outcome of the entire issue. Once the validity of the native land claim could be established in a court of law, it would help ensure the future of the island. History was made at Easter of 1984, at a festival in Tofino, when the Clayoquot Indian Band declared Meares Island a Tribal Park:

DECLARATION

Let it be known as of April 21, 1984, we the Clayoquot Band do declare Meares Island a Tribal Park.

1) Total preservation of Meares Island based on TITLE and survival of our native way of life.

2) Preserve Meares Island, as the island is an ECONOMIC base of our people to harvest natural unspoiled Native foods—including all:

A. Sea foods and shell fish.

B. Protect our traditional hunting rights of deer and water fowl, etc.

C. Protect the right of our elders to continue the gathering of their Indian medicines.

D. Protect the right of Native artists to continue the gathering of their needs. Cedar bark, cedar for canoes, and paddles and masks etc.

3) Protection of all salmon streams on the Island.

4) Protection of all herring spawning areas around the Island.

5) Protection of all traplines.

6)   Protection of all sacred burial sites on Meares.

The Native people are prepared to share Meares Island with Non-Natives, providing that you adhere to the Laws of our Forefathers which were always there. On this basis—we recognize your needs for:

A) Watershed, as they already have in place their water system on Meares Island.

B) Hunting of waterfowl in Lemmens Inlet.

C) Existing mariculture leases. We would reserve the right to process any further development, be it watershed or further mariculture leases.

We would permit access to the Island for recreational purposes—hiking, camping, fishing, whale watching, gathering restricted amounts of sea foods and shellfish.

Recognize our Land Claims and that there be no more resources removed from Meares Island, excluding watershed.

Signed by George Frank, (Hereditary Chief) Alex Frank Sr., (Hereditary Chief) and the CLAYOQUOT BAND COUNCIL.

Once the powerful declaration had been read and recognized, it ushered in a new era of co-operation. The enjoining of white environmentalists and natives strengthened considerably the conservation forces. With the vision of a native Tribal Park, each group involved would have a role to play. The community would never again look upon the issue in quite the same way.

Once the question moved into the courts, constant injunctions travelled back and forth between the parties involved: big business on one side, and natives and environmentalists on the other. Trips to court, involving long trips to Nanaimo, began to take a toll on this small family's resources—in every way. At this time, Linda and Michael were forced to re-evaluate their commitment, but decided they had come too far to turn back.

The many Friends of Clayoquot Sound remained firm and spirits were high. However, the fear of arrest was valid and forced parents to be realistic. Linda and Michael discussed every eventuality and decided that, when incidents arose, one of them would remain with the children, removed from the situation. In the summer of 1984 there was a civil disobedience workshop held, during which the principles of non-violent protest, in the spirit of Gandhi, were illustrated and discussed. The Friends became affectionately known as "tree huggers."

It was during these months of turmoil that Linda became even more acutely aware of the sanctity of nature and the perils incurred when man seeks to interfere, for reasons of his own. Young Jesse became ill. In the beginning he exhibited general malaise, then his small body became covered in angry looking hives. Within a short time his joints became swollen and extremely painful, to the extent that he was finally unable to walk. His parents took him to hospital where the doctors diagnosed it as chemical poisoning.

It was eventually decided, by a process of elimination, that the culprit was a bunch of grapes, bought in the local grocery store. The grapes had been imported from Chile and were later found to contain significant traces of pesticides. Linda had washed the fruit carefully but pesticides are impossible to wash off. The medical findings came as a shock to Linda. She found it hard to accept that, while she had endeavored to provide her family with a healthy, balanced diet, she had unwittingly been poisoning them. Jesse recovered, but his mother never forgot the frightening experience.

Linda began to read everything she could find about the dangers of herbicides and pesticides. She learned that, at certain levels, they could eventually cause nerve damage and even cancer. Living on the water, she was unable to cultivate a garden, so decided to order cases of organically grown fruits and vegetables from larger centres. She became interested in the healing properties of herbs, many of which were found in the region in which she lived. In the way of the true herbalist, she came to appreciate nature, not merely for its beauty, but also for the valuable resources of wild foods and medicines. More than ever before, she began to appreciate the environment around her as provider and teacher.

Through her discriminating use of herbs such as comfrey, arnaca, echinacea and garlic oil, she feels that she has strengthened the immune system of every member of her family. She finds the natural remedies gentle and non-invasive to the system. However, she doesn't hesitate to seek medical help when she feels the problem is beyond her. By the same token, on more than one occasion a local doctor has sought her advice on herbal theories. In keeping with the holistic principles which she has chosen to apply in all areas of her life, in common with her many native friends, Linda has given birth to her three youngest children at home.

In the summer of 1985, as the controversy over the fate of Meares Island raged, Linda set up a charter boat service which took people to the island. Nature trails were mapped out that permitted visitors to experience first hand the magic of walking in old growth forests, among centuries-old trees. She reasoned that no one who had actually walked among the giants would stand still for their destruction. Respecting the principles of a Tribal Park, a percentage of her proceeds was returned to the Clayoquot Indian Band.

So it was, that in the fall of 1985 when the logging of Meares Island seemed imminent, both Linda and Michael, together with other members of the Friends of Clayoquot Sound intensified their efforts to protect the island and its resources. Once MacMillan Bloedel chose the specific location the environmentalists began a system of ferrying local people to the site, where they camped on the shore. Some of the natives in Opitsaht had no boats, so supporters donated their time and their craft. Communication was maintained by the use of radio-phone. It was a tense time for everyone and emotions ran high.

On November twenty-first, boats loaded with loggers carrying chainsaws finally appeared in pristine C'is-a-qis Bay, prepared to begin the clearcut logging of Meares Island. Linda won't forget that cold morning when she received a call at the floathouse that the loggers were going in. She and her friend Susanne quickly mobilized people and boats. Then they collected their children and caught a ride to the bay on board the boat of an interested crab fisherman, passing the R.C.M.P. cutter on the way.

The mood at the bay was somber—tense but calm. Native people, together with environmentalists stood quietly on shore while in the water, a few feet away, the logging boat rested. In retrospect there was also humour. Someone was forced to ask the several members of the ever-present media to stand aside so that the long awaited confrontation could take place. The two groups met. The representative from the logging company stated the company's intentions and Chief Martin in turn welcomed the loggers to his land but requested they leave their chainsaws in the boat. After some quiet discussion a "gentleman's agreement" was reached, whereby, in a rather anti-climactic move, the loggers withdrew. The issue would be resolved in court.

Later, after months of archeological exploration to substantiate the native land claim, the concept of a Tribal Park was finally acknowledged by a court of law. Among the reasons stated for the decision was written: "It (Meares Island) is no ordinary logging site. It is an island with special values rising above commercialism. In a sense it is like a park. It contains trees of great size and antiquity. It discloses the history and culture of Indian Nations."

Further resolution of the land claim would involve many months, eventually years of involved legal maneuvering but for a time the island and its riches would be preserved. The legal costs to the native people continue to grow and in an effort to assist them in meeting their financial responsibilities, Linda and others have sponsored art auctions and other community events. The Meares Island struggle ushered in a new era in environmental activism. It has since encouraged people to recognize that the resources of the land belong to all people, not just to the few.

Linda says today that her motivation and her inspiration were, "The children, the generations to come, and the trees." As difficult as those times were for Linda and Michael and other members of the Friends of Clayoquot Sound, they would do it again, and in some ways feel fortunate. Many people in this world are concerned about the steady depletion of the world's resources and often feel frustrated that their voices are not heard. Relatively few however are presented with the opportunity to make a difference as did the tree huggers of Meares Island.

Recently eleven year old Jonathan Manson, a native child residing in Opitsaht, won an international haiku contest, with a poem written about his grandmother.

> *Meares Island*
> *Native mother*
> *picks healing tea leaves*
> *deep in the forest.*

NINE

The Common Loaf

As you walk down the hill toward the Government Dock in Tofino a delicious aroma wafts through the air: "Sugar and spice and all things nice" comes to mind. "Common Loaf Bake Shop" the sign reads, and as you enter, one of the first things you notice is an oversized bulletin board with food for thought. "As you sip your French wine and eat your French cheese, you might consider what France is doing in the Pacific," begins one article.

An announcement tells of a forum on Indian self-government and yet another invites you to a Celtic music festival. A press release from a British newspaper states "The situation at Greenham Common is desperate and urgent." There is a peace voter pledge card pinned next to an article from Amnesty International, and a notice for a Turtle Island Seminar. A map of Meares Island Tribal Park trails is tacked up on the board and several beautiful full-colour posters and post cards of Meares Island are displayed for sale. One particularly topical scene depicts the destruction of a British Columbia Forest by clearcut logging and the apt Shakespearean lines: "Pardon me thou bleeding piece of earth, that I am meek and gentle with these butchers."

To your right is the indoor seating area, defined by open-work wooden shelves and accented with healthy looking plants and graceful pieces of pottery. Guatemalan wall hangings decorate the shop and a small library of consciousness-raising literature is stacked for browsing. Behind the counter an attractive young woman is filling pans and placing them in the oven while another makes fresh coffee and yet another attempts to keep up with the demand for clean cups and saucers. Outside, the sturdy red cedar tables on the terraced deck are full, an eclectic mix of artists, fishermen, senior citizens, and children of the area, most of them regulars. The informal atmosphere reminds one of a friend's country kitchen. "Serve yourself and just put your money in the bowl," invites a friendly voice. It is then that you realize there is no glass in the showcase. The fresh fragrant Nicaraguan coffee is at hand, together with milk, brown sugar, honey, and herbal teas. A bake shop indeed, but, more than that, this hive of activity, on the main street of the village is a coffee house *extraordinaire.*

The idea for this bakery was conceived several years ago in a small village in Ecuador and reflects the commitments in life of its creator. Maureen graduated from Glendon College of York University in Toronto with a degree in social science and worked for two years as a caseworker in the inner city. She found it stimulating and challenging work but at times she felt almost overwhelmed by the misery she saw around her. In 1974 she decided to take a year off to travel, and perhaps find a new direction in life. She bought a van and set out to drive across Canada and down to South America. Shortly before leaving she noticed (in the old Star Weekly) a centrefold picture and accompanying article on Canada's newest national park, Pacific Rim, located on the west coast of Vancouver Island, and she decided to include that area in her itinerary.

It was love at first sight as she stood on the dock that first day in Tofino, looking out over the inlet backgrounded by mountains. The sea that day was a deep green, mirror-flat, and the combination was entirely soul satisfying. She stayed several days, camping in her van out at the park, taking long walks along the beach and spending companionable hours in conversation with other young people around the campfire in the evening. At night she went to sleep with the sound of the pounding surf lulling her to sleep. The beauty of the area and the freedom of the west coast lifestyle were new and exhilarating to this young social worker from the large eastern city. At some point during those few days, she remembers asking for a bakery, being told there wasn't one in the village, and filing that away in her memory.

Eventually she packed up her van and began her long journey south, through the United States and Mexico. She spent some time in Central America, crossed the Panama Canal, and continued into South America where she spent an unforgettable year meeting and living among the people of the various countries. She spent some time studying the co-operatives that enable small farmers to market their goods and often became involved with the women of each area, admiring their courage and resourcefulness, often in the presence of adversity and poverty. Her admiration for these people would stay with her the rest of her life and perhaps influence many of her decisions in the future.

It was on a late summer day in a small village in Ecuador, a village that sat overlooking an inlet backed by mountains and presenting a scene much like the Canadian west coast, that everything began to come together in Maureen's mind. After months of travel and exploration, not the least of which were her own boundaries, she suddenly knew what she wanted to do with her life. Soon she was on the road again, heading north.

Back home in Toronto, she explained to her family that she couldn't return to the life of the big city case worker. She had come to believe that there was something else that she was meant to do. "They thought I was mad." She made no promises, had no guarantees, and was equipped with only her sketchy high school cooking classes for experience, but within a short time she was driving back to British Columbia. This young woman was heading for Tofino…to open a west coast bake shop.

A few days and many miles later she drove into the village on a day in late October when she could scarcely see the rainforest for the rain. That fall, storm followed storm, but whenever a sunny day did present itself, the inlet and mountains would loom commandingly in the rain-washed light and Maureen would take this as a sign that she was meant to stay. During that winter she talked herself into a job as a cook for a local construction crew, having reasoned that this would give her access to an oven and also get her out of the van, as she would live on site. That first day she decided to serve the crew grilled cheese sandwiches and looked in vain for a cook book with the "recipe."

Her cooking skills gradually improved over the months and when spring came she decided to rent space in the newly opened "Gust O' Wind." This was a local performing arts centre with a unique concept, one that Maureen describes today as "slightly ahead of its time." Formerly the community hall, the two-story cedar shake building was located in the heart of the village and had been the scene of many a festive occasion over the years. It was leased from the village at a nominal sum by a small group of local artists and crafts people. The inside of the building was renovated and a series of tiny shops and studios were constructed, where people were encouraged to create in an atmosphere of camaraderie and mutual respect. The "Gust" became a centre for artistic development. More than that, it quickly became a gathering place for those of similar interests and aspirations, a small but committed community of young people. During summer months visiting artists from all over the globe would rent the small shops and there was an interesting exchange of thoughts and ideas.

Maureen's space was exactly that, and she set about transforming it into a miniature bakery. She insulated and then roughed in the walls with gyproc. Then she procured a second-hand kitchen range and hand mixer and for ventilation merely opened the small window. Finally, she had a Dutch door installed which provided her with counter space on which to place her "bakings." Since she couldn't both bake and wait on customers, she placed a graceful wooden bowl on the small counter for gross receipts.

From the beginning, her most faithful customers were her fellow occupants of the "Gust." Rather obscurely, she decided to master the art of baking rye bread, believing that once she could bake a decent rye loaf, the other products would seem relatively simple. The results of her labours were hard, brown little bricks which she, rather hesitantly, offered for sale. One of her friends, (the same artist who donated the wooden bowl) would dutifully buy one every couple of days. The price was mutually agreed upon. It was a price that today Maureen calls "highway robbery." Months later she asked him why he had ever bought the little loaves of hardtack and he told her that it had been his way of lending her moral support. He said he felt if he kept buying her products she would eventually learn to bake.

A friend from Toronto who was a dietitian visited the bakery soon after it opened and offered to send Maureen a couple of recipes as soon as she got home. Before long the fledgling baker was turning out bran muffins, banana loaf, and whole wheat bread. One day a neighbour contributed her recipe for chocolate chip oatmeal cookies, saying they were the family's favourite and she could never keep enough on hand. These basic items continue to form the foundation of this successful business today. During the summer months visiting tourists would swell the contents of the wooden bowl. There was one family from Vancouver with four small children who would visit every August and virtually clean out the little bakery. They still visit today, and even though the shelves boast many more offerings the family still cleans out the place.

During the years at the "Gust," Maureen became increasingly drawn into the web of west coast life. In 1980 she was

The Common Loaf

president of the arts centre when the village notified them that because of plans for expansion, they needed the building in order to relocate the library. The tenants fought to save it but to no avail. In August 1980 the "Gust O' Wind" was forced to close its doors.

At this time two friends purchased a building on First Street and offered Maureen commercial space. Her bakery would be the "filling" in a sandwich of three shops, and would be an exciting venture for the young entrepreneur. It meant moving "uptown," a distance of three blocks. It also meant that the next few months were very busy.

Once again, her shop was bare wall space. There were many trips across island and over to the mainland to locate reliable second-hand equipment. She had to purchase commercial-sized ovens, mixers, and fans. Once again she drew up plans and began to build shelves, cupboards, counters and a small showcase. These tasks the social worker cum baker cum (of necessity) architect and carpenter accomplished with a great deal of hard work, some financial maneuvering, and "more than just a little help from my friends." The fact that she had never used professional equipment before prompted Maureen to spend a two-day apprenticeship at a very accommodating bakery in Victoria. They also shared with her their recipe for peasant bread, and, with some slight alterations, this bread has become a west coast favourite. The next step was to hire the bakery's first employee, another young woman who had worked in a bakery in Montreal and shared her knowledge with Maureen. The new "Common Loaf Bake Shop" opened its doors on Good Friday, 1981.

From the beginning, the friendly little shop began to fulfill some of the functions of the "Gust." It became the meeting place for the do-ers and the thinkers (known in other milieu as the movers and the shakers), and the creative people of the area. Maureen increasingly became in touch with segments of the community, both native and white, who until then had no common meeting place and all were made to feel welcome. Indeed, many would say that this bake shop/coffee house has been, and continues to be, more in touch with the west coast spirit than any board room or council chamber.

In 1979, both Maureen and her husband John, local teacher and dedicated conservationist, became founding members of the "Friends of Clayoquot Sound." From that time on the bake shop quite naturally became a rallying point for environmentalists and, during the winter months, when the Friends office was closed, it served as unofficial headquarters. Not only did it become the financial centre, where donations were left and sales of various arts and crafts were held, with proceeds going to fund the Meares Island protest, but it was the place where information was passed and strategy was discussed.

Much like the Speaker's Corner in Hyde Park in London, the bake shop became a mecca for free and democratic speech and action and a haven for those prepared to stand up and be counted for their environmental beliefs. For several years Maureen has been a director of the "Friends of Clayoquot Sound." In that capacity she has helped sponsor environmental seminars and speakers, including David Suzuki, and helped fund studies and books on the area. One of the most positive aftermaths of the hotly contested Meares Island protest—when west coasters stood shoulder to shoulder was that today the native people feel comfortable in the bake shop. Indeed, they are some of its best customers.

These days, during the busiest season, the bakery has a staff of thirteen, and all are assets to the business. Many of them work part-time because out in this part of the world everyone needs their beach time. With yet another move has come the attractive outdoor seating area. While the bakery is larger, the atmosphere has not changed. The open baking area, the casual seating space, and the original wooden bowl testify to that. One person, a trained baker, works the night shift and her entire time is spent making bread. Another comes in early to prepare for the 8:00 A.M. opening. The emphasis has always been on top quality whole earth ingredients such as whole wheat flour, cold-press safflower oil, and island honey. Many of these come from health food suppliers and co-operatives. Cakes and cookies, squares and buns are baked all day long to keep the showcase filled. Even so, in the tourist season the cheese and cinnamon buns can be gone by noon and the bread by 3:00 P.M. causing grumbling by the local people.

In recent times Maureen's life has taken on new direction. During the summer of 1988 when, during the Sulphur Passage stand-off, concerned citizens were once again called upon to stand firm for their environmental beliefs—sometimes in the face of very real danger to themselves—Maureen came to a decision. By this time she had become increasingly aware that a large segment of the local population had no political representation, no voice with which to speak on vital environmental issues. She reasoned that along with environmental activism must come the power for change, and that until such time as sincere and honest concern was backed up by political clout, their hard won gains could be lost or weakened.

It was a concept whose time had come. Maureen won a seat on the village council with a resounding majority and her presence on that illustrious body has been as a breath of salt air to some, while to others it has more closely resembled sand in the shoes. She has found it to be an interesting experience, one that has been challenging, frustrating, exciting and rewarding. She is learning that much of council's work is tedious and time-consuming, but is determined to consider everything from re-zoning proposals to building permits with a view toward what will benefit her community in the future.

Toward this end, Maureen was the guiding force behind a recent seminar held in Tofino regarding sustainable development in Clayoquot Sound. Highly respected experts in the fields of aquaculture, forestry, fishing, and tourism formed the panel, along with a representative of the First Nations, chairman of the Nuu-Chah-Nulth tribal council. Not only were they present as guest speakers but all participated in the well-attended work-shops and spirited debates that followed.

It was the first time that the various groups, each with a vested interest in the area, had sat down together to voice their concerns and put forward proposals. Without exception the representatives expressed a willingness to work together, to trust, and to accommodate. To all but the most cynical, a new spirit of co-operation seemed to be putting down tentative roots. The most dramatic event occurred at the end of the seminar when Simon Lucas, a local chief, invited to deliver the closing words, stood to address the packed gathering.

In slow and measured tones the man began to relate some of the changes he and his people had experienced over the years, from the time the stewardship of the land had passed from the Indian to the white man. He told of spawning streams destroyed, over-fishing, and the pollution of the sea. He described the catastrophic effects on his people when their surrounding environs, much of it magnificent first growth forests upon which they were dependent for much of their sustenance, were reduced to moonscapes, the steep mountainsides razed down to the edge of the sea. The room was hushed, the audience in the palm of his hand. Finally, he implored the people present to realize that time was running out. Once the benevolent giants of the forest were gone, we would not see their like again. "Man must learn to live in harmony with all creatures under the sun and to recognize that that which we do unto the most insignificant being in the universe, we do unto ourselves."

On my most recent visit to the bake shop, I found Maureen (literally wearing her baker's hat) icing two large pans of squares fresh from the oven. She was being enthusiastically assisted by young son Lee, while around them the staff moved at their usual frenetic pace. In one corner a young woman was selling colourful, handcrafted jewellery, while in another sat a young native couple, the mother unobtrusively breast-feeding her baby.

Just inside the door sat two men I knew to be oyster farmers, intently hunched over a game of chess. I took my coffee and cheese bun outside to the deck where I sat enjoying the panoramic view of Meares Island while around me swirled a microcosm of west coast life.

On the street the familiar vans were parked, the owners taking a break at their usual time, at their usual tables. Dogs as large as black bears lounged outside. Small children played near the tables and a fisherman carried a brown box of still-steaming bread down the hill to his boat. Three local women sat in the shade on the bench in front of the shop, as comfortable as if in their own back yards.

Maureen joined me at the table with a roll of blueprints in her hand. Once again her expanding business was necessitating a move, this time to her own building. We studied the plans for the new structure destined to be built just up the street. It would become a landmark in the village. A spacious shop, complete with traditional cupola, widow's walk, and trade mark deck. A credit to its multi-faceted owner.

I remembered Maureen explaining to me the meaning behind the name of the bake shop: "The common woman is as common as a loaf of bread—and both shall rise."

TEN

Ladies of the Lights

Since the days of the early Greeks—when bonfires were lit on cliff tops to guide their ships at sea—lighthouses and their keepers have been, for many people, objects of mystery and romance. I am no different. An invitation to visit the Lennard Island lightstation had been extended to me several times, but in order for one to make a safe landing by boat all elements of the maneuver must be in harmony: sea calm, winds light, and visibility excellent. Finally the call had come from the station and I was on my way. I met Tony, the lighthouse keeper, at the Coast Guard station at 10:00 A.M. on a picture-perfect day in June and we headed around the point in his 16-foot Zodiac, past Felice Island and out into Templar Channel. We then raced—with bone-jarring speed—through the light chop, past tiny Tonquin Island toward Lennard, a distance of three miles due west of Tofino. He slowed the boat as we threaded our way through the gap, blanketed at this time with heavy beds of kelp.

Tony's wife Margaret and I had been corresponding for several months and I caught my first glimpse of her standing, in her rubber boots, on the algae-slick steep cement ramp, scattering crushed shells from a pail, much as a farm wife would throw feed to her chickens. As the boat moved closer on the crest of an incoming wave, and at a signal from Tony, I launched myself over the bow of the vessel and onto the shell-tractioned ramp. Tony tossed my light travelling case onto the ramp and then piloted the small boat back to the centre of the gap and clamped it to the cable that swung overhead, climbed into an even smaller dinghy and rowed it back to the ramp, stowing it well above the high water line. Then he climbed the stairs to the winch house built halfway up the cliff, started the diesel engine, and the Zodiac was slowly airborne up the face of the cliff. Margaret, waiting above, guided the boat to its resting place on a trailer atop a concrete pad. Arrival procedures (precarious even in the best of weather) taken care of, the three of us continued up the steep stairs and over a small bridge to their house.

It was a sturdy three bedroom bungalow. The large kitchen led to a comfortable living room whose walls were lined with bookcases and which contained an organ, television set, and a V.C.R. Margaret showed me to the bedroom I was to use, formerly occupied by their son Stephen, where once again the walls held bookcases and on the desk sat models of sailing ships and a small telescope. The third bedroom had been converted to an office and boasted a state-of-the-art word processor. Back in the kitchen again, we sat down for lunch while the intermittent broadcast of Coast Guard information over the radio-phone beside the table formed a counterpoint to our conversation. Suddenly a familiar voice came through the air waves and we hurried to the window to catch a sight to stir the blood: a graceful double-masted schooner, the *John Muir* (named for the nineteenth century naturalist) beating a passage past Wickaninnish Island in the distance.

After lunch Margaret invited me to explore the light station and its environs at my leisure. Lennard Island, named for an English sea captain, is a rocky little island comprising seventeen acres, partially covered with second growth red cedar and traversed on the east side by a gully. In earlier days marine traffic was heavy along this stretch of the west coast, which came to be known as the "Graveyard of the Pacific." Ships from the Orient, carrying exotic spices and silk, as well as people wishing to settle in the New World, passed sealing schooners bound for London with cargoes of superb furs, and the ever-present whalers.

Vicious storms blew many a ship off course and onto the reefs, with an appalling loss of life and cargo. More than four hundred shipwrecks have been documented, one of the more recent being the *VanLene* in 1972. The 8,354 ton Panamanian registered ship, bound for Vancouver from Japan with a shipment of three hundred cars had been deflected by the northbound Davidson current and went aground on Austin Island in Barkley Sound in heavy fog. During the ensuing investigation, it was revealed that the captain had steered the entire trip by hand compass! So it was that the Lennard Island lightstation became a vital link in the chain of man-made coastal defences against the sea.

The buildings stand on cleared land facing out to sea, with virtually no land mass between them and Japan. The light tower, most commanding feature of the island, rises from the highest promontory and its beam can be seen for many miles. The other buildings are on a lower level and are afforded limited protection from storms. All the buildings sparkled in their coats of white paint and contrasting scarlet roofs. Seen from a distance they appeared as if assembled out of LEGO blocks by some giant child. Borders of meticulously raked white rock surrounded the houses and were interspersed with small green bushes, pink tea roses, and the occasional red bench. Two large vegetable gardens were neatly laid out. Below the homes, at the edge of the water, stood the helicopter pad. The advent of the helicopter has transformed life for families on the lights. As I made my way between tall hedges cut from the brush, past the second house (empty at this time, awaiting the arrival of the new assistant keeper and his wife, due in four days), I was struck by the lushness of the small island. A huge honeysuckle bush—festooned with chandelier-shaped blossoms and attended by honey bees—perfumed the air and I had literally to dodge hummingbirds in my path, while in the distance a fox sparrow split the silence with joyous song.

Tony offered to accompany me on a trip up the tall cylindrical light tower. Stepping through the door at the base, we began our slow even climb up the tightly coiled staircase until at last we stood outside on the small platform, nearly 150 feet above the level of the sea, our backs to the huge lens. The panoramic view from that vantage point was truly breathtaking. To the north lay the islands of Wickaninnish and Vargas, to the east Meares and the Esowista Peninsula, and to the south Long Beach. Walking around to the other side, we gazed westward to the horizon, which curved under a cloudless blue sky, presenting indisputable evidence that the world indeed is round. Later, back on the ground, Tony showed me his album of pictures taken during the construction of the present light tower. It was built in 1987, a scant few feet away from the previous one. Work crews and supplies were brought in by boat and helicopter to erect this triumph of modern construction techniques. The former one had been made of fibreglass and had the disconcerting habit of swaying slightly in strong winds. The final pictures showed the old tower being lifted off its foundation then flown away, dangling beneath a large helicopter. It resembled a gigantic filter-tip cigarette.

That afternoon Margaret and I sat around her kitchen table and shared a pot of tea. Margaret was born in Lancashire, England, one of seven children and the only girl. She attended a convent school and after graduation obtained her business diploma. Seeking adventure, she and a girl friend, Brenda, set off for the United States where they worked in New York and Los Angeles.

Welcome to Lennard Island

On a holiday to visit Brenda's aunt and uncle in Victoria, Margaret met and fell in love with Tony, Brenda's cousin. A year later, following Tony's release from the Canadian navy, they were married in the bride's home town of Preston. Soon after, the couple moved to New Zealand where they lived for two years. Returning to Victoria, Tony applied for a position as lighthouse keeper, having fond memories of visits to a lightstation as a child.

He was accepted and his first posting was to Chrome Island, located in the Strait of Georgia, off the east coast of Vancouver Island. At that time their first child, Stephen, was four months old and the little family travelled to the island aboard the Coast Guard icebreaker *Camsell*. They were transferred from ship to shore by means of a Bell 47 bubble helicopter—their first trip aboard a helicopter, and one that lasted a mere two minutes: a means of conveyance that would become increasingly familiar over the years. After nine months on the lightstation situated off the southern tip of Denman Island, Tony was transferred to Bonilla Island, south of Prince Rupert in Hecate Strait. The island lies east of the Queen Charlotte Islands, directly in the path of the ever-present pods of killer whales, colonies of sea otters, and luxurious cruise liners, full of curious tourists. Then to Cape Scott, one of the most northerly, cruelly isolated lightstations on Vancouver Island, inhabited largely by seabirds. One year later the family was again relocated, this time to Ivory Island near Bella Bella on the mainland, for five years. Finally, they were transferred to the west coast of Vancouver Island, to Lennard Light, where they have remained since 1974.

Raising two children on the lightstations of British Columbia has had its share of challenges over the years for both Margaret and Tony. Fortunately both boys were healthy babies, although Margaret always had handy a well stocked first-aid kit and her book on child care by Dr. Benjamin Spock, patron saint of many lighthouse children. The only family emergency occurred when David received a deep gash on his knee, while playing on the rocks. The lifeboat was dispatched from the Coast Guard station in Tofino and he was removed to hospital where the doctor sutured the wound and sent him home. Due to return a week later, rough seas made the trip impossible and so Margaret got out her kit, sterilized her fine manicure scissors, and did the job herself. Another time, a young assistant died suddenly of a heart attack and a doctor arrived to attend to him via life boat within half an hour.

One of the most important and far-reaching decisions parents on the lights must make is how their children will be educated. Margaret and Tony decided to home-school the children through correspondence courses, rather than send them away— either to boarding school or to live with relatives. This meant the lessons consumed much of Margaret's time during the early years until her young sons were of an age where they could read and understand the directions. Hours of schooling conformed closely to the norm, with a certain amount of flexibility. A sunny day, coming after days of rain, prompted a closure. The arrival of a helicopter, or the supply boat, bringing mail, guests, or provisions, liberated the boys for an instant recess. Many a science experiment was performed in the family kitchen and some produced rather startling and messy results.

Margaret admits that one of the most difficult aspects of this regimen was the necessity of separating, (both in her mind and those of the boys) mother from teacher. As part of their extra-curricular activities the boys produced "The B.L.I. Papers," in which they detailed their lives on Beautiful Lennard Island, often setting their compositions adrift in bottles. They had several replies, one from a fellow student living far to the north on the Aleutian Islands. Regularly their physical education period consisted of a game of softball, with Tony as pitcher and Margaret as back catcher—when a smartly hit ball could be lost to the waves lapping in the outfield.

Their days were full, although on occasion, when housebound for several days due to inclement weather, the boys insisted to their parents that the fog horn spoke to them of BOOO-OOOO-RING! As the boys grew older the family took leave twice yearly, usually amid the bright lights of Victoria. Today David is in the navy and Stephen recently earned a Bachelor of Science Degree at the University of Victoria. He is now working toward a Master's Degree in astronomy at McMaster University in Hamilton, Ontario.

The days of a lighthouse keeper's wife are busy—not only with children, but with planting a large garden and preserving its bountiful harvest, baking and sewing, and cooking for the work crews that arrive regularly. However, most feel that it is important to do something for themselves. Margaret began working toward her Bachelor of Arts degree ten years ago. She took correspondence courses from the University of Waterloo, studying in the evenings when the house was quiet. She majored in classical studies and particularly enjoyed her courses in the history of music. Unable to attend her convocation exercises, she recently received her degree through the mail. Coincidentally, Stephen was home for a short visit at that time and Margaret prepared a special "convocation dinner," complete with champagne. Mother and son toasted each other's accomplishments while Tony looked on with pride.

Retirement, due in two years, has become the subject of much planning and discussion and, while both Margaret and Tony have enjoyed their years on the lights, they are looking forward to new experiences. These will run the gamut—from building their first home and owning an automobile again to such small luxuries as visiting a library and attending concerts. Margaret privately wonders if they haven't developed a "drawbridge mentality" as she calls it, and expects they will need to relearn some socializing techniques. Unlike most women however, one aspect of retirement won't require adjustment—that of having her husband around all the time.

In the absence of an assistant keeper, Margaret was taking the watch that evening and I accompanied her on late rounds.

With flashlights in hand we made our way to the building that housed the communications unit, engine room and other sophisticated equipment—the so-called nerve centre of Lennard Light. Both the rooms and the machines they contained were spotlessly clean. We donned ear mufflers and entered the engine room where Margaret checked the generators, making sure there were no oil leaks. Next she set the fog detector on automatic (so finely tuned, she explained, it was often triggered simply by a high moisture content in the air) for the hours between 11:00 P.M. and 3:00 A.M. when Tony, who had retired early, would rise to take the early watch. We entered the communications room and precisely at 10:40 P.M. Margaret lifted the receiver and prepared to relay present weather conditions to the Coast Guard station in Tofino.

First we heard Pat's voice giving the weather from Nootka light further up the coast. Nootka lightstation, built in 1911, stands on a rocky headland at the entrance to Friendly Cove, one of the most historic locations on the west coast. It was here that Captain Cook landed in 1778. I had met Pat and her husband Ed when they visited Victoria a few months earlier. She explained it was her first visit to the city since 1981, the year that saw, among other events, Indira Gandhi sworn in as Prime Minister of India, the appointment of Jeanne Sauve as first woman speaker of the Canadian House of Commons and the death of Ingrid Bergman. Rather than feeling deprived, however, Pat couldn't wait to return to her beloved Nootka. Only the necessity of medical appointments, long delayed, had drawn Pat to the city. She mentioned that she never felt as lonely as when she found herself among groups of people in the city and that she longed to return to the freedom and familiarity of her island home.

Born on the saltchuck (Pender Harbour) Pat has been on the lights for more than thirty years—longer than any other woman in British Columbia—and freely admits, "When I can't hear the ocean I become a little strange." Like Margaret and Tony, Pat and Ed raised and schooled two children on the lights. Their son Dean is a paramedic and addictions educator living in Vancouver. Daughter Nicalena recently married a logger and lives close by in Kyuquot. Once the children were older, Pat began to take on increasing responsibilities.

For several years Pat has operated the communications desk during the lonely night hours. During this time, many a seaman, calling in for information or perhaps a friendly chat, has come to know Pat's warm husky voice. Some of the men have shared information about their families, their ups and downs, their aspirations, occasionally even asking for advice. A warm camaraderie has developed with some although, ironically, the two will probably never meet face-to-face.

We had discussed many aspects of lighthouse living, from the delicate matter of maintaining good relations with other staff—under circumstances that preclude the luxury of avoiding a person with whom one has personality conflicts, to the pressures that living on a remote station can put on a marriage. Pat cautioned that an isolated lightstation is not the place to go to attempt to rejuvenate a faltering marriage. She felt the isolation can enrich a strong union but it can also destroy a shaky one. She also warned that isolation can do strange things to a person's inner resources. It can be a blessing for those who discover new strengths and abilities, but it can be a curse for those who, despite determined effort, never quite adjust.

On the subject of the policy of de-manning lighthouses along the coast of British Columbia, Pat was forthright in her opposition. She cited the rescue work instigated and carried out by lighthouse keepers and their families, working as a valued component of the Coast Guard. She felt they play an essential role in assisting the people who "go down to the sea in ships," by monitoring sea and weather conditions several times daily. She also mentioned the good will extended to the many visitors to the more accessible stations throughout the years. Once the services are fully automated and the families gone, the proud maritime tradition of the keepers of the lights will be irrevocably altered. Pat and Ed can't quite envision life anywhere but Nootka and will be facing some difficult decisions in the future.

In the communications room, the next voice on the phone detailed weather conditions from the station on Estevan Point, long regarded as British Columbia's most bold and beautiful light. Completed in 1909, it is an eight-sided monolithic column, braced by graceful flying buttresses, which rises 150 feet in the air. Its original classical lens—painstakingly assembled and shipped from Scotland—was the largest ever placed in a light tower. This architectural giant graces one of the most beautiful sites on the coast. It also has the dubious distinction of having been shelled during World War II, allegedly by a Japanese submarine, although many subscribe to the theory that the attacker was actually an Allied ship, in an attempt to outrage the Canadian public and speed the passage of the conscription bill before parliament in Ottawa. Pauline and Joe spent eleven years at Estevan, electing to leave only recently in order to forge new careers in the face of gradual de-manning of lightstations.

Pauline describes her life during their years on the lights as "moving in rhythm with the seasons." Summers were busy dealing with the many visitors to the station, whether they were hikers traversing the convoluted west coast or boaters anchored off shore. The constant refitting of the station came to a peak during the warm weather and Pauline's days grew even busier as she provided room and board for the work crews arriving at regular intervals. In fall, it was back to the classroom for the mother/teacher and the two children, Cindy and Sam. It was also time to preserve the abundant harvest from her large garden and often Pauline worked at this in the evenings when the children were in bed and Joe was on watch. Before the advent of the helicopter, winters were relatively quiet months, but in recent years even winters were filled with activity. Spring brought the return of the whales, the hummingbirds, and the blossoms, events that are all too often overlooked in the city.

Pauline misses her walks along solitary beaches with her dogs. She recalls their years as keepers at the station at Chatham Point, on the inside passage, north of Campbell River. There, from their kitchen window, they used to watch killer whales engaging in playful displays on the traditional "rubbing beaches " below. In retrospect, both Pauline and Joe look back on the time spent on the lights as the best years of their lives. However, she cherishes her new-found freedom in the city (Victoria) and the challenges of attending college and working toward a business degree.

Back on Lennard Island, evening rounds accomplished, Margaret and I made our way back to the house and prepared to retire, secure in the knowledge that should an emergency arise during the night, Tofino Coast Guard Radio would alert them by means of the loud buzzer on the lighthouse phone beside their bed.

The next morning I woke early, to the muffled but insistent boom of the fog horn, a mere 200 yards from my pillow. Outside lay a completely different world from the one experienced yesterday. The island lay as if wrapped in grey, damp, cotton wool: the buildings and light tower had disappeared without a trace. Catching a whiff of freshly brewed coffee, I pulled on my clothes and hurried to join Margaret and Tony in the brightly lit kitchen. While enjoying a hearty breakfast, the three of us paid close attention to the radio description of the weather system rapidly moving into the area and I began to wonder if my departure from the island might be delayed. Shortly thereafter however, we became aware of a capricious breeze that had begun to worry the edges of the fog until it fell back to reveal sunny skies and a benevolent sea. Fearing this might be a short lived respite, my hosts left to prepare the Zodiac for launching and I hurriedly gathered my few belongings.

After the enactment of a complete reversal of landing procedures, the Zodiac was brought bobbing to the ramp, as if eager to be off. Margaret and I had time only for a quick hug and promises to keep in touch before Tony helped me scramble into the boat and we were moving through the gap. Turning, I had one last glimpse of my friend Margaret as she waved, standing outlined against a dirty grey wall of fog that threatened to envelop her. Back in Tofino I was deposited at the Coast Guard station and Tony made a quick turn around to beat the fog back to Lennard Island.

Two hours later the rain began falling, gently at first, then settling into an unrelieved downpour. The rain continued with few respites over the next ten days, sending many tourists scurrying back over the mountains in search of the sun. At night out my window I could see the strong beam from Lennard circling the peninsula and during the day the sound of the fog horn constantly accompanied my activities, providing both a feeling of reassurance and, in the most pleasing of ways, communication.

I often think of those gallant women who work alongside their men on the lighthouses of British Columbia. Creating a home, raising and educating her children under circumstances that would defeat many of us, each has moulded her own particular lifestyle and wouldn't trade her isolated outpost for the finest mansion in the city. Even though most have met only over the air waves, theirs is a close and caring sisterhood, built up over the years. As for me, my visit to Lennard Light only enhanced the romance of the lights.

ELEVEN

Strawberry Island

For months I had watched the activity on and around the tiny island that is within hailing distance of the village: the children rowing to school in the morning, in fair weather and foul (much like children of earlier days), divers making practice dives in the surrounding waters, the wind surfer launching his colourful craft from the shore, and the constant small boat traffic to and from the island. I wouldn't forget that winter day I had watched in horror as a small seaplane, attempting to take off into the teeth of a gale, was tilted off course by a particularly vicious gust of wind and dashed against the reefs.

Sharon and Rod and family are the sole human inhabitants of Strawberry Island—a rocky little island that is indeed shaped like an inverted berry—situated in the middle of the Tofino harbour. In the centre of the treed island rise three tall silvered trees, long dead, whose snags are home to a family of bald eagles. On the promontory, facing the village, sits their home, the *NorVan* 1, original ferry that plied the waters of Burrard Inlet between Vancouver and the north shore from 1900 to 1925. This vessel, bought years ago as a derelict, has been lovingly restored and serves as a unique home to the family of five.

Sharon and Rod arrived in Tofino as newlyweds nearly twenty years ago, determined to make a life for themselves on the west coast. It was a hot dusty day when they drove into town, with all their worldly possessions, including their large black Labrador dog, crammed into their dilapidated van. Rod was born and raised in the mining town of Trail, far from the sea. As a young boy he read books by Jacques Cousteau in which the world famous marine scientist detailed his studies beneath the surface of the ocean. There were vividly coloured illustrations accompanying the text, showing a world hitherto unknown and Rod decided that, somehow, that was what he wanted to do when he grew up. When he left school he moved to Victoria where he worked at various jobs, and with the money earned he began to educate and equip himself for the intricacies of deep-sea diving, a method he doesn't recommend to anyone. It was there that he met seventeen year old Sharon and after a short courtship the two were married.

During their first months on the west coast they lived in their van out at the beach and Rod worked as a diver, harvesting geoduck clams. Eventually they found lodging in a building that had served as a barracks at the Long Beach airport during World War II. They partitioned the second floor and, with one of Rod's friends, established a maritime museum with artifacts gleaned from local collections, which they supplemented with specimens Rod uncovered during his dives. Sharon performed most of the curator's duties, listing and cataloguing the items and displaying them attractively in glass showcases.

When Sharon became pregnant the couple decided to look for a place of their own but the housing situation in the small village was very tight and nothing was available. It was at this time that the *NorVan* entered their lives. It was owned by a local crab fisherman who anchored it off a nearby island and used it as a float-

ing machine shop. By then there was very little of the super structure left. When the owner died, the boat was to be sold for scrap.

In typical west coast fashion, friends of the couple
helped raise the necessary funds to purchase the derelict vessel.
Next, the machinery was auctioned off and the job of reconstruct-
ing the proud old ship began. Working from original blueprints
and photographs they found in a museum, Rod and interested
friends painstakingly brought the vessel to life again. It was an
exciting day when the *NorVan,* former ferry, was refloated as a
family home, in the lee of Stone Island, in Clayoquot Sound.

Thus began nearly ten years of living on the water.
Years that saw the arrival of five children, with each child's name
establishing their link with the sea. "Waterbabies" their friends
called them, and Coral, Gil, Pearl, Fion and Shell flourished in
their marine environment. Rod was often away and, of necessity,
certain ground (or rather, water) rules were laid down and these
were strictly adhered to. The children grew up in the protective
second skin of their life jackets. In the way of all children, however, despite all precautions they managed to cause their parents
many an anxious moment. Sharon recalls how, more than once,
she rescued a youngster who had, in the enthusiasm of the
moment, ridden his tricycle off the end of the deck and into the
ocean. One of the most frightening occurrences was for them to
wake in the black of night during a storm, to an insistent thump-
ing against the hull of the ship. This was invariably caused by a
drifting log and it was imperative to quickly locate it and send it on
its way before it drove a hole through the framework. At the
height of one memorable storm in their small cove, the merciless
winds completely flattened Rod's workshop on deck.

During these early years Rod sought to establish an
ocean salvage business, hoping to demonstrate how, in many
instances, it was more economical and efficient to employ a diver
rather than unwieldy cranes and grappling devices. He realized
that the new technique would take time to become an established

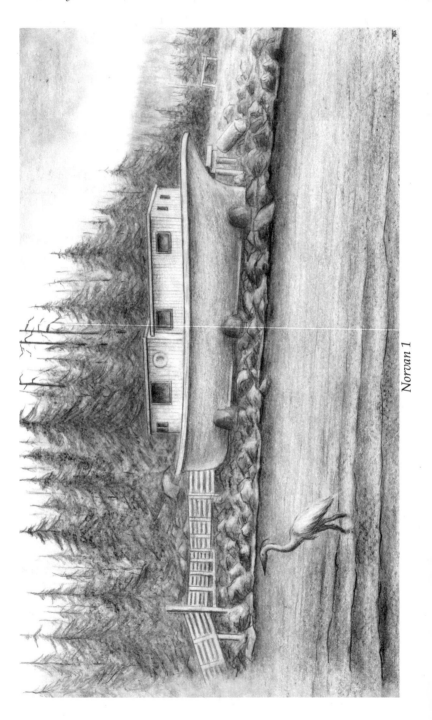

Norvan 1

practice. One of his first jobs, in 1975, involved the salvage of the four hundred ton, three-masted schooner *Hera,* which burned and sank in fourteen fathoms of water off Clayoquot in 1899. Part of the cargo had been sixty thousand bottles of Rainier beer, packed in oak-staved barrels. Rod recovered several of the casks and today many a household in the area boasts at least one of the bottles. The large anchors from the ship stand in the village square.

Over the years Rod has salvaged everything from the M.V. *Solander,* supply vessel for the outer coast, to helicopters and fishing boats that have met with disaster. However, one ancient wreck has so far eluded him. The whereabouts of the trading ship *Tonquin,* sunk in Clayoquot Sound in 1811, remains a mystery to this day even though various archaeological dives have been made in an attempt to find the richly-laden vessel. Over the years he has also become a skilled underwater photographer, with examples of his artistry displayed in many books about the sea.

Between salvage jobs Rod worked as a sea harvester, diving for sea urchins, abalone, and clams, to supply the oriental market. As a result, Sharon was often alone on the boat with the children, a radio-phone her only means of outside communication. With the toddlers securely wedged in the bottom of the craft, she travelled by canoe to the village in order to buy groceries and do the family laundry, often visiting friends' homes for coffee and "the quickest shower in town." This unorthodox manner of living was made all the more remarkable by the fact that, at that time, Sharon didn't know how to swim and had a definite fear of the water.

The years afloat were good ones and each member of the closely-knit family, no matter how young, grew to be resourceful and self-reliant. In 1980, when their mooring lease came up for renewal, Sharon and Rod gave it some thought and decided instead to purchase Strawberry Island, which would place them closer to town. At that time the island was owned by a man in Alberta whose wife had nearly drowned off its shores, and he was anxious to sell it. The deal was completed and the *NorVan* was floated across the inlet to the island. Next began the herculean project of raising the eighty-three ton ship from the surface of the ocean to its permanent home atop the promontory facing the village. Some said it couldn't be done, but once again, friends conferred, the family supplied the work force, and together they began the task. Slowly and laboriously, working with the tides, they would first jack up the prow of the ship one foot and secure it, then do the same with the stern section. And so they proceeded in this simple manner, applying the most basic of engineering principles, and the venerable *NorVan* slowly began to leave the sea and move over the jagged rocks, to finally become a part of the island. The undertaking took a year, and when it was finished the family had one of the most unusual homes on the west coast.

Over the years Sharon and Rod have made the island uniquely their own. It has become a meeting place for people with similar livelihoods and interests. In time certain traditions evolved, from the summer pot luck barbecues where the menu may boast everything from pickled geoduck clam to marinated octopus, to the Christmas eve carolling party, when the voices drift across the water to the village.

Since first coming to the area, Sharon has found fulfilment in her roles as wife and mother and also as Rod's helpmate and partner in all his endeavours. It is a source of pride to her to see the children, as they grow, begin to train and work alongside their father. (Today Coral is a well known folk singer and works in the environmental and peace movements.) However, as they matured and became more independent, Sharon began to look for new challenges. A few years ago she took a job at the local hospital.

Some of her most rewarding moments came when working as a labour coach assisting the doctor in the delivery room. Women began to request her presence during their confinement. She would often fly into neighbouring villages as part of the medical team.

Then came the years of disruption in Clayoquot Sound, when clearcut logging began to imperil a way of life. It was impossible to live in the area without being drawn into the situation that threatened to turn neighbour against neighbour, native against white. The family became involved in various activities designed to support native land claims. Sharon joined her friend Linda in setting up a charter boat service that would enable people to visit Meares Island and experience first hand the magic of time spent in an old growth coastal rainforest—an experience limited only by the depth of a person's sensitivity.

I visited fabled Meares one morning during the early fall. Five of us made our way down to the small dock where Sharon met us in her 24-foot Boston Whaler. My companions were a young couple from Germany and two film makers from Sweden, commissioned to produce a documentary on Canadian west coast rainforests. Sharon was accompanied by the family dog Tonquin (a regal mix of Alsatian and wolf) who became our figurehead at the prow of the boat as we headed up Lemmens Inlet, the wide, picturesque waterway dotted with small islands dividing the northern arms of Meares Island. The diaphanous morning mist still hovered lightly over the water, while across the harbour Lone Cone loomed tall, wreathed in cloud. As we slowly moved over the surface of the water, the mist broke into small, ghost-like patches that wafted off over the land, as if in search of refuge. The morning warmed, the light intensified, and the island began to reveal itself in all its dramatic splendour.

As we drew near the landing site, cameras were checked and light meters adjusted. After giving each of us a map of the island and the nature trails it contained, Sharon set a time to meet us on another beach later in the day and then left us to explore the island, each in his own way. The others moved off at a purposeful pace while I, absorbing my surroundings with every pore of my being, slowly made my way along the trail, which was marked with yellow ribbons.

The deeper into the forest I hiked the more sensual the experience became. The growth was luxuriant, exuding the fragrance of musk, that enchanting bouquet of the forest distilled from pine needles, cedar, fungus and decaying humus. I was aware that cougar, bear, and wolf inhabited the island but somehow the knowledge seemed entirely welcome rather than threatening. At that time of year mushrooms were plentiful and grew in various sizes and colours, from white to red, and beige to violet. Fungus growths—snow white and some as large as dinner platters—jutted from the trunks of trees. No fall colours here, this forest was resplendently green and sparkled with miniature, dew-spawned rainbows, while bright red salmon berries winked through the dense undergrowth like nature's mini-lights. Silver-green moss hung from branches in spongy clumps and when I rested against a tree my hand sank into its softness. In this primeval sanctuary even the air seemed green and I was as a child in the garden of Meares.

Further along I stopped to rest at the base of an ancient Sitka spruce. The silence lay heavy: no birds flew in here and no birds sang. The sun filtered through the branches in vertical shafts and I lay on my back on the spongy forest floor in order to see the tops of the trees, outlined against a deep blue sky. The serenity of my surroundings soon engulfed me and I slept. When I woke, I continued on, traversing a sylvan meadow at the edge of an estuary and fording a small creek that would be, once the rains came, teeming with spawning salmon. I eventually met up with my companions in a glade of ferns and salal, beneath an alder, close to the beach. Conversation seemed superfluous in our surroundings, we were still listening to the echoes of the voices of the forest.

A few months later, on an unseasonably warm February morning, I had an opportunity to visit Strawberry Island. Sharon picked me up at the Crab Dock and as we approached the *NorVan* I was able to appreciate the old vessel's new coat of warm red cedar. It was already beginning to weather to the silvery sheen that any self-respecting west coast dwelling must have. Once aboard, we sat over steaming mugs of coffee in the comfortable galley in the stern of the ship, doors flung wide to admit the sun. Beyond the uncurtained windows, the normal commerce of a bustling seaport went on around us at its usual frenetic pace. A large dredger worked opposite and vari-coloured fishing boats and water taxis gave texture and motion to the scene. Sea planes took off and landed closeby, their occupants often waving cheerfully as they skimmed past the island. From inside the *NorVan* it was difficult to remember that we were not actually afloat.

We moved to the prow of the vessel, to the former saloon, a large room that is the focal point of many family activities. One wall consisted of a large mural depicting subterranean life, while others were hung with art prints and photographs, including a sepia-toned photograph of the *NorVan* during the height of its importance as a freight and passenger carrier. (The *NorVan* began life as a steam powered ferry built by the North Vancouver Ferry and Power Company in 1899. A solid vessel of wooden construction, it is 73 feet long and has a 20 foot beam.) The curving windows welcomed the forest inside to become an integral part of the home's decor, and a large mobile, crafted by Sharon, from various shells found on the island's shores, hung from the ceiling. The space designated as Rod's office was lined with nautical manuals, various maps and marine charts, books on photography, and classic novels of the sea.

In one corner of the room sat a wooden rocking chair which Sharon described as their barometer. The family has grown accustomed to riding out rough weather in their ferry home but occasionally during the winter, when the waters rise, threatening to refloat the vessel and a sou'easter roars down the inlet, causing the windows to vibrate, the old chair will begin to rock of its own volition. It is at these times that the family, believing that discretion is the better part of valour, will temporarily abandon ship, making an orderly withdrawal to the wood shed.

After lunch I accepted Sharon's invitation to explore the islet. Back in the trees, overlooking the harbour, stood the 15-foot statue of Weeping Cedar Woman. The figure, carved by a local artist, became the symbol of the spirit of Clayoquot Sound during the early days of environmental activism in the area. Her hand was raised in supplication and wooden tears streamed down and over her suckling breasts. Further on, out on the point, sat a pair of crossed anchors, salvaged from some ancient galleon and closeby stood the large weathered skull of a grey whale. I continued along the rocky shore, past a dugout canoe which I knew Rod and Sharon sometimes filled with children, and went exploring. I crossed a minuscule beach at the site of the recent plane crash and continued walking until I reached the far side of the island. I began to climb, and soon stood on the summit which afforded me a spectacular view of Lemmens Inlet. It was here that the sisters from Clayoquot had planted terraced gardens and taken tea many years earlier. Their beloved rhododendrons are now growing wild on the island. It was low tide and several blue herons fed on the sand banks, at first glance seeming to walk on the water, while on a nearby reef, sat a group of cormorants, resembling a coven of witches.

I suddenly had the feeling I was being observed, and looked up, straight into the glittering eyes of a large bald eagle, seated in the snags above. He surveyed me, disdainfully, for what seemed minutes, then lifted off, circling over the island then moving off up the inlet. Sharon had explained that over the years the family has come to have a very special connection with the eagles who make the island their home. More than once an immature eagle has been injured and the family has nursed it back to health, building a pen to contain the fierce bird until it can be released into the wild. Often the eagles will follow the family boats, circling above and soaring in the updrafts.

Back aboard ship I found Sharon donning her floater coat, preparing to leave to pick up two men for a trip to their fish farm further up the inlet. As we left the island we passed the children rowing home after school and Sharon slowed the whaler to tell them what time to put the clam casserole in the oven if she were delayed. After a quick good bye on the dock she left with her passengers and I walked slowly back to my lodging.

Strawberry Island and its inhabitants are some of the colourful strands interwoven into the tapestry that is west coast life. During the day the island reflects the many moods of the inlet, while at night the warm lights at the stern of the ship beam across the harbour, a presence in the darkness. Perhaps most spectacular of all is the magic moment coming after a shower when the clouds lighten and suddenly a rainbow is seen straddling the island. It is a natural phenomenon so utterly charming that one begins to wonder about that pot of gold at the rainbow's end.

TWELVE

Kakawis

The cold grey rain had continued unrelentingly for the last three days and I had decided to start the day with a hot breakfast to drive the chill from my bones. The early crowd having thinned, the hotel dining room was deserted except for a slim young native woman who sat at the adjoining table with a battered suitcase on the floor beside her. As we waited for our orders to arrive we struck up a conversation in that oasis of warmth and light. She introduced herself as Maria and volunteered that she was waiting for the bus back to Nanaimo. There she would transfer to another coach line that evening to begin the long journey back to the Queen Charlotte Islands and what she hoped would be a new start in life. She asked if I'd heard of a place called Kakawis and when I told her I'd been invited to visit sometime in the future, her face lit up. She invited me to sit at her table where, over a platter of bacon and eggs, she began to share her story with me.

To begin with, she said, her mother and father had both been alcoholics and both had denied the painful truth up until the day they died. Knowing this, she now felt that her own catastrophic problems with alcohol had been pre-ordained. She also said that she was determined not to follow in their footsteps any longer. Maria was the youngest of three children. She hadn't seen her sister and brother for many years: in fact she had lost contact with them and by now had no idea where they were or even if they were still alive.

Years ago, at the age of ten, without any prior warning, she'd been precipitously removed from her Haida parents' home on the reserve and sent to a residential school in southern Alberta. It had happened so quickly she hadn't had a chance to say goodbye to anyone or to take even one personal possession with her. For many months thereafter she thought she was being punished for some misdeed, one she couldn't even remember. No one thought to explain to the young girl that it was simply government policy at the time. It is now seen to have been a misguided policy, one that literally kidnapped native children from their homes, sent them far away to school, and attempted to recast them in the mould of the white man. It would rob a whole generation of native children of their heritage. Indeed, it was not only a policy doomed to failure, but one that would wreak havoc on an untold number of native families.

Maria's first year at the school, run by a Catholic charity and staffed by lay Sisters, had been torture. It was as if the young native child had been transported to a foreign country. The first night, curled up in a bunk bed (one of forty in a large dormitory room) among strangers, Maria cried herself to sleep. In the morning she was lined up with the other girls and her long glossy braids were snipped off. From that time on she was forced to wear her hair in a boyish cut—for reasons of cleanliness she was told. She was obliged to change her name, formerly Laughing Eyes, to Maria. The children were issued grey uniforms and heavy black stockings; the material, starched to a boardlike texture, irritated the skin and the stockings never seemed to fit. The students were prevented from having any contact with their families during the school year, not even at Christmas. They were forbidden to speak their Indian language, even among themselves, or to play Indian games in the school yard. Theirs was a "dead culture" they were repeatedly told. Even the food was different. Maria, used to living largely on fish and other products of the sea, venison, corn, and fresh berries, grew to loathe the starchy macaroni and cheese served four times weekly and the grey, tasteless mush that constituted breakfast seven days a week. Even today, the smell of peanut butter can turn her stomach.

Maria made a friend that first year. Teresa, who had arrived at the same time from a reserve near Fort St. John, proved to be a soul mate. Teresa was the same age as Maria and the two displaced children became inseparable. The girls ran away twice in the first few weeks. The first time they attempted to hitch-hike to Calgary but were spotted on the road and returned to the school by the R.C.M.P. The second time they managed to get on a Greyhound bus headed for Edmonton but returned voluntarily when they found themselves penniless and at the mercy of street toughs and the hostile prairie winter. Both times they were punished by having to spend a week in a little room under the eaves. The time was to be spent studying the Bible which they did, but they also spent much of the time singing their Indian songs and playing simple Indian games. Both girls were almost sorry to see the punishment end and, once they returned to the routine of classroom life, spent much of the time surreptitiously planning the next break for freedom.

Each summer, the students were allowed to return to their reserves—provided their parents sent money for a bus ticket home and signed a paper promising the child would return for classes in the fall. That first summer, Maria couldn't wait to get back to her beloved home by the sea. She fished with her brother, ran free in the woods, didn't wear a stitch more clothing than was absolutely necessary, and let her hair grow. Often in the evenings she would sit with her grandmother around a fire on the beach, while the older woman taught her the ancient songs and related stories handed down to her by her grandmother. Maria often visited her mother's sister nearby. Her aunt was known for the beautiful beaded moccasins and jewellery she created and sent south to be sold in the tourist centres. On occasion she would let Maria work alongside her at the kitchen table. When they stopped for supper, she would make a point of preparing Maria's favourite dishes.

By the time the second summer finally came, her grandmother was dead and both her parents were drinking heavily. During the third summer her parents were killed during a storm at sea. It was later determined that they had been drinking while fishing and had not been able to outrace the sudden squall. Her aunt, having no children of her own, made way for the orphaned child in her home but things were never quite the same again. Shortly after Maria returned to school that fall, her brother landed in jail, having knifed a companion during a drunken brawl, and her sister headed for the bright lights of Prince Rupert, with her two year old son. Maria stayed at the school during the ensuing summers.

Finally, at the age of seventeen, both Maria and Teresa were permitted to graduate. They were each given twenty-five dollars and a bus ticket home. It was Stampede time in Calgary and as they waited for their connecting bus headed west, they got talking to some young men who invited them to a party at a house somewhere in the south-east end of the city. There were many young people there that evening—some were dancing to loud music from the radio, others were sitting in a circle smoking and laughing while others congregated around the kitchen table playing cards and drinking. The next morning Maria woke to find herself in bed with two men, neither of whom she remembered. She looked for Teresa but couldn't find her—she never saw her again. Teresa's body was found by the side of a country road the following spring.

Kakawis Dock – Welcome!

Nine months after that fateful party Maria gave birth to a baby boy. She hadn't even realized she was pregnant until the contractions began. By this time she was living in the house, usually sleeping on the floor, and managing a day-to-day existence, dependent upon the kindness of the various occupants, none of whom stayed long enough to care. She made a point of maintaining a low profile, staying out of the sight of authorities. Her constant companion during these months was alcohol—beer and cheap wine, usually supplied by others.

After the baby arrived she was determined, with the help of a social worker, to put the city life behind her and return to her former home in the Queen Charlottes. She got as far as Vancouver, when the baby, whom she had named Running Deer, sickly since birth, suddenly died of pneumonia. By this time she was pregnant again and staying with new friends on a reserve just outside the city. She continued to drink and was delivered of a stillborn child in her eighth month of pregnancy.

The shock of this second death awakened in her an overwhelming urge to somehow turn her life around, before it was too late. An Indian social worker had been assigned to her at that time and this woman followed Maria's progress with the persistency of a terrier. She found her a job doing dishes at a nearby native drop-in centre, and there Maria met other young people with stories similar to her own. Over the next few years she worked at various jobs in the city, most of them low paying, demeaning jobs. Somehow she managed to keep a roof over her head and food on the table during those years. She never lost sight of her goal to eventually put the city behind her and return to her home by the sea.

It wasn't until one final impulsive drinking bout with new-found friends, one that put her in hospital and nearly took her life, that she was able to accept her powerlessness over alcohol and humbly turn her life over to a Higher Power. Her social worker arranged for her to go directly from hospital to Kakawis, the native centre located on the west coast of Vancouver Island. After having spent six weeks there, she was going home to her beloved Haida Gwaii, a journey begun many years ago. Maria was determined to find and re-establish contact with the remnants of her family and, at the same time, to chart a new course for her own life. She hoped eventually to work among her people as a social worker or a nurse.

The rain had slackened somewhat and I helped Maria load her suitcase onto the bus. It was odd to think that I hadn't known her a scant two hours earlier. We hugged goodbye and I stood and watched the bus disappear down the road. I knew I wouldn't forget Maria, with her luminous eyes and long glossy braids. I felt her at my side some weeks later when I visited Kakawis—that place of hope—across the water.

It was shortly after sunrise on a beautiful crisp winter day when I boarded the school boat at the Fourth Street dock in Tofino. Kakawis Family Development Centre has risen, phoenix-like, from the ashes of Christie Indian Residential School on the shores of Meares Island. Christie was the realization of the life-long dream of Father Charles Brabant, much loved missionary who worked amongst the west coast Indians for many years. The school was named for the Bishop of Victoria who allotted funds for its construction. It opened its doors to the surrounding native population in 1900, an outstanding example of European architecture and European values. The large edifice resembled a castle, set amongst the evergreen forest of the rugged Canadian west coast. It was, in some ways, a stately, cream-coloured anachronism.

In the beginning, Indian families were, understandably, reluctant to send their children to the white man's school. The original enrollment, in the first year of the twentieth century, was disappointing to the Oblates. However, they had faith, and, when the first group of students returned home, they brought with them knowledge—knowledge of the white man's way—which, for all its imperfections, was the way of the future. Native parents began to accept the benefits of this new way until eventually being a graduate of Christie became a point of pride among the people.

Approximately ten thousand native children would pass through the beautifully hand-carved doors of Christie, nurtured and educated by Catholic Oblates and Sisters. For many of the newly ordained educators it was as new and curious an experience as it was for their students. Christie grew and flourished. Not only did the school have a solid academic programme but their athletic teams were second to none. Their appearance at Clayoquot Days always ensured spirited first class competitions. More than one young athlete unofficially equalled a world record. Christie's band and choir were equally in demand. Among the happiest occasions was the return of former students to be married in the ornately beautiful chapel. And so it was that all west coasters mourned when beloved Christie burned to the ground in the summer of 1979.

The trip from the wharf in Tofino to Meares Island that crisp winter morning passed all too quickly. As we sailed, Pat, the director of the family centre, explained that one of the meanings for the name Kakawis was "place of many berries." We moored alongside a small pier where a hand-painted sign proclaimed: "WELCOME. WE ARE GLAD TO SEE YOU PEOPLE." The meaning of this greeting became increasingly clear as the day progressed. We followed a path through the forest, across a small bridge newly constructed over a meandering creek, to the bluff, which overlooked a crescent beach and sparkling bay, a picture-post-card-inspiring scene.

Kakawis has become an alcohol and drug abuse rehabilitation centre for the native people of British Columbia. It is unique in that it specializes in the treatment of the whole family—which is together from the first day of the entire six week encounter. The centre takes a holistic approach to addiction, a way of living common to Indian communities. An emphasis is placed upon getting to know and feeling comfortable with oneself. It stresses the importance of love, of being honest with oneself, and

143

of making choices in life. A basic aspect of the philosophy is learning to live in harmony with all of the natural world, becoming one with the elements around us. It is a very spiritual programme.

Today was a special occasion for the families in treatment, a culmination of six weeks of sharing, learning, and growing. Never again would they be alone with their problems. Pat and I began the day by participating in the sweet grass ritual. We became part of a group of eight people seated in a circle around one who kindled the wild grasses and passed the receptacle to each person. This sharing represents the symbolic cleansing of the mind and body. The sweet-acrid fragrance filled the silent room while hands clasped and prayers were offered. The power of the circle is always very strong and very supportive. Pat and I soon slipped away, leaving the group to express final private feelings and thoughts.

Outside, the day continued to warm, and Pat offered, with justifiable pride, to show me around the grounds. Hiking trails had been cleared to the sea, the fresh water lake, and the summit of Lone Cone—the gentle rounded mountain of volcanic origin that has loomed over Clayoquot Sound and its peoples for all of living memory. My senses were assaulted (in the best possible way) by this surfeit of nature. A bald eagle perched in the snags of a tall cedar tree, the adjoining bay was rich in clams I was told, and the many wild berries would soon be fat and juicy. There was a feeling of anticipation about the place. Recently wolves had been observed approaching the clearing, a most auspicious omen in Indian legend. Little wonder this island holds a significant place in west coast history.

The participating families were once again becoming in touch with nature and slowly beginning to uncover the proud core of their "Indian-ness." This was being encouraged to happen in totally supportive and compassionate surroundings, among new and understanding friends. Sadly for some, it was the first time they had ever been able to feel pride in themselves and their race.

At noon there was a farewell buffet dinner in the social centre, the heart of Kakawis. Small groups of women made their way to the building, most with platters of food in their hands. Pat was carrying a plate of muffins that his wife Colleen had baked the evening before, regretting that he had forgotten to take the butter out of the refrigerator in time to allow it to soften. Inside the long hall the men had set up rows of tables and chairs the length of the room. The mood around the tables was relaxed and happy. Former graduates, additional family, and friends had arrived by now, to share in this day. After a blessing, expressed by the drums, we sat down to a munificent meal which consisted of everything from smoked salmon, freshly harvested clams and oysters, rice and vegetable casseroles, to layer cakes and lemon meringue pie. Toddlers squirming in high chairs and young children laughing gave a homey atmosphere to the occasion.

After the meal we freshened up and then returned to the social centre. The tables were gone and the chairs had been placed against the walls. Up until then, I'd been conscientiously recording facts, dates, and statistics. Included was a quotation from a non-native member of a study team: "Indians have taken the leadership in the whole area of prevention and treatment. They have done a lot more than non-Indians over the past twenty years." Also included from the same study was the statement: "Much of the native population of British Columbia lives in small communities and/or in conditions of deprivation, so that the health and social problems of native people are more visible than the health and social problems of most other British Columbians." Having attended a local, non-native British Columbian social function the previous evening, one where "spirits" were enthusiastically raised, I could appreciate those words. At this point in the day, as the Blue Bead ceremony was about to begin, I put away my ridiculous note pad and began to truly experience some of the magic of Kakawis.

A glass bead of cobalt blue had been given to each client the previous week. In earlier days, the Venetian cut glass beads had been brought to the shores of the northern Pacific by Russian traders eager to barter with the native people for their premium furs. And so the precious beads became units of commerce and part of Indian culture. Here at Kakawis the bead symbolizes the trading of one's former life for a new and more meaningful one. Each person was requested to fashion a necklace or bracelet, to be exchanged with another from a fellow journeyer down this, the new road. Faces were strained now, voices lowered. It was much like preparing for a final examination in feeling, honesty, and love. Everyone present was aware, however, that the ceremony marked, not a "final" but a beginning.

What followed next was one of the most beautiful communions of the human spirit that I have ever been privileged to witness. One by one the couples came together briefly to express to each other their hard-won understanding of the past and their hopes and commitment for the future. The final couple, two young women, parted after a final clasping, and there was the five year old daughter of one, sitting silently crying. She was very much aware of what a change was about to take place in her life. Everyone was hushed and I sensed that more than one of us had to restrain ourselves from going out to Violet, wrapping her in our arms, and hiding our own brimming eyes in her hair.

An hereditary chief, his wife and family present, expressed with heartfelt eloquence how much the Kakawis experience had meant to them. They then distributed beautiful, handmade gifts to staff and new-found friends. Next, while their children pounded the drums and sang, John and Trudy, in traditional dress, led us all in a dance of celebration. This helped us release some of our pent-up energy and emotion. Pat spoke briefly of the value of "washing the mirrors of our inner beings with the healing water of tears" and told us, men and women, not to be ashamed of these emotions.

All too soon, after hurried farewells, the group that had arrived in the morning had to set off down to the waiting boat. Good natured jokes were made about "our" hereditary chief (and counsellor) having to get back to Tofino to make supper for his young family. His wife, also an addictions counsellor, was attending a two week seminar. A chief's work is never done apparently. Had it been only ten hours since I had set foot on these welcoming shores?

The sun was setting behind Catface Mountain—one of those extravaganzas of colour that catch one completely unaware in the winter—as we threaded our way among the small islets, through water suddenly stained apricot. During the crossing, I thought back to two letters Pat had read to me in his office that morning. They came from a man who detailed his activities and those of his wife, both of them former clients, since returning home to their reserve in the interior of the province. They had immediately begun to translate their Kakawis experience into positive action.

They started by describing to anyone who would listen, what had transpired in their lives. They also showed films, answered questions, and finally helped sponsor a dance. This was the first "dry dance" ever held in the village, and most people attended out of a sense of curiosity rather than from a conviction that they would have a good time. To their surprise they actually did have a very good time and could remember every detail the following morning. No apologies were needed for words or deeds that might have offended their friends. The second letter, from the same man, spoke of accepting an offer by the R.C.M.P. special constable, himself native, to run the films. The couple had become increasingly busy setting up referral and counselling services and helping sponsor more "dry dances."

Early the next morning I thought of the families leaving the island, that gentle place, that place of dignity, and travelling home, to take up life once again in their villages. It would be challenging, frustrating, and difficult. It could also be exciting and rewarding. It would not be unusual for them to experience all these feelings and emotions on any one day. I also thought of

Maria and silently wished her well. Something would sustain them in most instances. They would be able to return to Kakawis—in their hearts.

THIRTEEN

Whale Song

Early on a summer morning in June, I met Shari and
Robert and two year old Sirena at their waterfront home near the
Coast Guard station in Tofino. After a quick cup of coffee, Shari
took Sirena next door to stay at a friend's home for several hours,
during which time she would be measured for a wet suit, surely
one of the smallest ever made. The three of us pulled on bright
yellow floater suits and picked up our binoculars and cameras.
Shari hung the "Gone Whaling" sign in the window and we set
off down the dock to where a 30-foot Zodiac sat bobbing in the
water. The couple were to guide a C.B.C. film crew the following
day and were going out to survey the surrounding waters before-
hand. The busy little port was already humming with activity. We
passed several vessels headed for the fishing grounds, the school
boat bound for Kakawis, and a herring skiff loaded with colourful
plastic barrels, to be used as floats on an oyster farm. We continued
up Browning Passage, the body of water that separates Meares
Island from the Peninsula. It was down this same picturesque

waterway that the early settlers used to row to Clayoquot for supplies.

We soon entered Grice Bay, where Robert cut the motor and we drifted silently…waiting. Suddenly, about fifty feet to our starboard side, the waters parted and a barnacle-encrusted leviathan—the great grey whale of the Pacific—surfaced, eyed us curiously, then effortlessly made its way toward us. With Robert snapping pictures, both Shari and I leaned over the rubber boat to stroke the giant mammal but, before we could make physical contact with it, another grey broke the surface nearby and blew, its fetid, fishy breath drifting over the boat. The two began to swim closer to shore, diving at intervals to feed along the bottom.

While we followed at a respectful distance, Shari explained that these whales had broken away from the main body of migrating whales in the spring and seemed content to spend the summer feeding in the waters of Clayoquot Sound. It was low tide by now and along the mud flats that bordered the inlet there was much activity: a family of river otters sunning themselves on shore, mink running along a log, and the flash of a white-tailed deer. At one point, as we stopped while Shari checked a friend's oyster lease, we saw starfish of various colours, from metallic blue to orange, winking through the clear water like jewels of the sea.

Finally, Robert started the engine and we turned for home. As we passed a rocky outcropping near Indian Island we noticed several fat sleek seals, motionless, appearing as part of the rock. As we drew nearer they suddenly reared up as one and a concerted yelping filled the air. Just then we saw a killer whale, dorsal fin erect, cleave the water, with all the power and speed of a locomotive. The seals frantically scrambled for safety but one was too slow. By this time the whale had launched itself out of the water and dragged the seal, squealing, below the surface. For a short time the water churned and turned red and then there was silence. It happened so quickly and violently that I was shaken, even though I realized that it was simply a graphic example of the laws of nature. We continued to scout the channel, under the watchful eyes of several bald eagles who soared effortlessly in the updrafts around us. Finally we turned for home in time for my hosts to take out the first boat load of whale watchers.

Gifted ballerina and professional stage actress, Shari came to the west coast via Mexico, Central America, the Galapagos Islands, and many points between. Born a free spirit, under the sign of the Pisces, she has absolute faith in her psychic sensibilities—"I have lived many lives." She gave up a promising career as a dancer to live aboard her 32-foot charter boat the *M.V. Kitgard* and operate a whale watching business on Canada's west coast. In recent years she has become a respected authority on marine mammals, in particular the great grey whale of the Pacific.

Shari grew up in Chatham, Ontario, a small city situated midway between Lake St. Clair and Lake Erie, and some of her happiest times were spent aboard the family boat, sailing with her father and older brother. Both her mother and grandmother had been professional dancers and her mother ran a school of dance. At an early age, petite Shari displayed exceptional promise in her mother's classes and it was assumed that she would follow in the family tradition.

At the age of seventeen, after graduating from high school with honors, Shari expressed a desire to seek a university education rather than follow in her mother's footsteps as a dancer. Her parents told her that if she chose such a course she would do so without any financial help from them. She obtained a scholarship to Ryerson College where she majored in classical ballet but also carried a full academic schedule. During her college years Shari managed to support herself by earning a succession of bursaries and scholarships and also by appearing in various stage plays and musicals. As a mark of her professionalism, she became a full-time member of Actor's Equity.

In her final year of college she was awarded the lead role in the school's year-end dance review. One night, unbeknownst to the young dancer, famed Anna Wyman was in the audience. After the performance she visited Shari backstage and—stuff of dreams— offered her a position in her distinguished dance company in Vancouver. To Shari it was a dream come true and she accepted at once. Shortly after graduating she flew out to the west coast, prepared to sign a contract and get on with her life in show business. When it came time to sign, however, she discovered to her dismay that, rather than the adequate salary she'd anticipated, the company paid only her travel expenses. As she was being offered a full-time position, it would be impossible to supplement her income. Reluctantly, Shari was forced to snatch defeat from the jaws of victory.

Heartbroken, and practically penniless, she wandered the streets of the city where, in the best tradition of Hollywood musicals, she met in a bistro that very night, a young man whose brother, a doctor, required a medical receptionist. Very soon thereafter, she was reorganizing the doctor's office, bringing in a healthy salary and maintaining a toe-hold in the dancing world by guest-teaching at the prestigious Pacific School of Ballet. She rented a quaint little shack on the beach at White Rock, south of Vancouver. Life went along smoothly until one day she noticed a picture of her funky little home in the local paper under the heading "BULLDOZE and BUILD." She decided to pool resources with a friend and buy a boat. Chris was an experienced sailor and the two young people finally found something that fitted their requirements. The merchant vessel *Kitgard* was a sturdy wooden boat, built in 1937, whose heart was a Gardiner engine, worthy of respect in any marine community. After three years of living together on the water, Shari and Chris separated and she bought out his share in the boat.

At that point Shari pulled up anchor, set sail for Vancouver Island, and moored the *Kitgard* in Brentwood Bay. She worked at various jobs around Victoria, living on her boat and becoming an amateur boatwright in the process, thanks to the generous help of other boaters moored nearby. One of her favourite jobs was waitress in the coffee shop at Canoe Cove. She felt that under its roof, at any hour of the day, was assembled more knowledge of matters marine than any other place she had ever been. The young woman listened and learned.

Eventually however, she grew restless, and one day answered a newspaper advertisement placed by a man who was seeking a crew member for a yacht, to be delivered to the buyer in San Francisco. She moved the *Kitgard* to Vancouver where she left it in the care of a friend, and was off. She couldn't know it at the time but she had begun her own personal voyage of discovery, one that would last two years and take her thousands of miles. It was an odyssey that would test her every resource as she sailed in an assortment of motley vessels with a succession of skippers who displayed various degrees of competence and mental stability. Her first skipper proved to be a gruff, uncommunicative man and Shari spent much of her time trying to avoid him—not easy to do on a 40-foot boat. She looked forward to her turns on watch, when she took the opportunity to play her guitar and write songs.

It was on this initial segment of her journey that Shari had her first close contacts with the creatures of the sea. They were experiences that she never forgot, and they awakened a desire within her to explore the mystique of communication between humans and marine mammals. One afternoon, as she sat out on deck, a school of bottle-nosed dolphins began to follow the boat. As it pitched to one side, her bathing suit, which had been hung to dry, fell into the sea. Immediately a dolphin caught it on his snout and proceeded to tease Shari with it, staying just out of reach until finally swimming away with his prize, much like a mischievous child. Another day a huge sun fish swam alongside the boat, then languidly turned and waved its fin, as if in greeting. One starry night when Shari had the watch, a whale surfaced closeby in the inky darkness and blew, and the swishing sound was "like the breath of God." She found it strangely calming, as if the whale were letting her know she was not alone.

Upon arrival in San Francisco, rather than returning to Victoria as she had originally planned, Shari signed aboard the *Cosmic Dancer.* This time her skipper was a delightful senior citizen, skilled sailor, cultured gentleman, and fellow vegetarian. His boat contained an extensive library and a wealth of music. The two quickly became friends and Shari was sorry to see the trip end in San Diego.

By this time cruising was in her blood. She had become a fledgling member of the "fraternity," those who roam the seas of the world and whose direction in life is ruled by the turn of the tide and the pull of the wind. She next crewed for a couple and their two sons, week-end sailors all, aboard a sailboat bound for Mexico. It was during this voyage that she first observed the mating of the grey whales. When they reached Acapulco Shari found employment in a yacht club.

Three months later one of her customers told her he was looking for a crew member to help sail his boat to Costa Rica. For one of the few times in her life Shari ignored the warnings of her "inner voices" and lived to regret it. She was getting restless again and was ready to move on. It was the beginning of hurricane season in that part of the world but they decided to make a run for it as the weather forecast was encouraging.

Once they were underway, it became obvious that this skipper was dangerously inexperienced. The boat wasn't even trailing a dinghy, for emergency use. To make matters worse, on the second day the winds died, leaving the boat becalmed in the doldrums: "The longest ten days of my life." Shari spent most of her time on deck trying desperately to keep her spirits up. It was during this period that Shari began to feel that the actions of the dolphins, who stayed near the boat for long periods mirrored her moods whether they be depressed and anxious, or upbeat and hopeful. By now the skipper had become morose and withdrawn, keeping largely to his bunk. Finally, one morning their sails filled with wind and they were on their way.

While they were still off the coast of Mexico a hurricane struck, with mountainous seas and demonic winds. The skipper panicked, leaving control of the foundering craft to Shari. At the end of the first day, as the storm grew in intensity, Shari recalled the words from Joshua Slocum's book *Sailing Alone Around the World*, when he had found himself in a similar life-threatening situation. She set about securing everything as best she could, including tying the lines from the mast to the boat so the mast wouldn't be lost if the boat rolled. She recalls seeing an amazing sight as she worked frantically. Two enormous marine mammals, the largest she'd ever seen, (to this day she is not sure what they were) were surfing down the huge waves behind the boat, as if at play, and somehow the sight reassured Shari. She went down below and tied the skipper to his bunk and then did the same for herself. There was nothing left to do at that point but pray. In the morning they woke to calm seas. (In his book, Joshua Slocum also woke to a calm sea, but noted that his fish cleaning knife was embedded in the deckhead, or ceiling, proof that the boat had rolled over completely at least once during the night.)

As they approached the coast of Costa Rica another storm struck and this time they were lucky to escape with their lives. At the height of the storm, the skipper decided to make for a small bay to try to ride out the turbulence. Shari felt instinctively that the attempt was doomed to failure but couldn't dissuade him. He threw out the anchor but the force of the waves continued to pull the boat toward the rocky shore, where by now a small crowd had gathered. One young man swam out to assist them and Shari threw him her sea bag which contained most of her worldly goods such as passport, money, camera, her journal, and the songs she had written. He ferried them into shore, one arm held high above his head, and then returned for her precious guitar. For eight hours the storm continued to slam the boat against the beach until at last they were forced to abandon her.

Once safe on shore, after twenty-one days at sea, (a voyage that would ordinarily take ten) they were given dry clothes, a hot meal, and lodging. The next morning, at low tide, a huge crane was used to salvage the boat. Shari spent three months in Costa Rica and came to love the gentle, selfless people. The skipper also stayed and eventually married one of the local women. Being fluent in French and Spanish opened doors for Shari and, once again, she found a job in a local yacht club. Shari found Costa Rican society to be largely matriarchal, the women being well educated and leaders in the community.

She became friends with an older couple (who, incidentally, were nudists) and they offered her passage aboard their yacht to Panama. This proved to be a leisurely, idyllic voyage. They often moored just off-shore, dove for food from the sea, and collected coconuts from the trees ringing the beaches. In the early mornings natives would often approach their boat in dug-out canoes filled with fresh fruits and vegetables for barter. Their favourite items were fish hooks, notebooks, pens and pencils and…tins of American spaghetti.

In Panama Shari met a man who was en route to Ecuador to purchase a boat to sail to Tahiti. By this time she had heard tantalizing tales of the fabled Galapagos Islands and reasoned that this could be an excellent opportunity to visit them, so she flew south with him and a boat was chosen. The vessel, although decrepit and of questionable vintage, was judged seaworthy and off they set. Time revealed, however, that once again Shari was adrift with a week-end sailor and the bulk of the navigational chores fell upon her shoulders. At the end of eight days open ocean sailing they glimpsed Galapagos on the horizon.

As soon as the boat was safely moored off-shore, Shari lost no time rowing herself ashore in the dinghy. She was met on the beach by a frisky little black dog "who seemed as if waiting for me." The dog led her down the beach to a large two-room cave on the site of a dilapidated whaling station. She was welcomed inside by a friendly little man in his seventies, the so-called "King of Galapagos." Gus had sailed from Germany before World War II, settling in Galapagos. The islanders had, over the years, come to love him and accept him as their spiritual leader. The cave contained a fire pit, two complete whale skeletons, and furniture made from the bones of whales. The walls of the caves were covered with quotations from many of the world's greatest philosophers, from Goethe to Shakespeare. There was an instant rapport between the young woman and the old man, "as if we had met before, perhaps in another life," and they talked for hours.

Shari obtained permission (rarely given) from the port captain to stay on the islands and was given a house to live in. For three months she worked aboard an American research vessel, studying the Bryde whales of the area. This valuable experience served to further her interest in the behavior and communicative skills of marine animals. One day, just as the native islanders were beginning to hint that she would be welcome to marry one of their own and settle on the islands, she met two Swedish friends whom she'd known in Costa Rica. They were leaving the next day for San Francisco and she signed on as crew member. Thus, the final leg of Shari's two year journey at sea ended aboard a luxurious 65-foot Hatteras power boat. The hot showers, microwave, and television were a treat but the most welcome feature in Shari's eyes was the automatic pilot!

Back in San Francisco, her payment was five hundred dollars and a plane ticket to Vancouver. Once again adrift in the city, in a Rip Van Winkle scenario (most of her friends' conversation revolved around mortgages and moppets), she found it difficult to adjust. She lived aboard the *Kitgard* which showed the evidence of two years of neglect, so she set about restoring it to its former state of sea worthiness. Then she began to do charter work. A call came in from Tofino requiring a boat for use by a crew constructing a fish farm. Shari responded, sailing up the outside coast of Vancouver Island in the fifty year old *Kitgard* which performed beautifully. The boat remained on-site in Irving Cove for seven months, during which time its diminutive skipper did everything

Whale Watching

from feed the crew to help construct the holding pens for the fish. However, when a road was blasted through to the area and clear-cut logging began on the slopes surrounding the picturesque cove, Shari decided to move on. She found the sight and the sound of the centuries-old giants of the forest being torn from the earth very disturbing, and the images never left her.

She decided to move down the coast to Tofino and, once there, she moored the *Kitgard* at the Fourth Street Dock, fifth finger, and set up housekeeping with her handsome cream coloured malamute Chief and her white cat Splice. This location afforded her an excellent opportunity to once again commence the study of marine mammals.

Every spring, over twenty thousand grey whales migrate in the waters along the west coast of Vancouver Island, travelling north to their summer feeding grounds in the frigid waters off Vancouver Island. They return along the same route in the fall to their calving grounds in the warm lagoons of the Baja Peninsula, southern California—an annual journey of 10,000 miles and the longest migration of any mammal on earth. Grey whales are bottom feeders, preferring tiny marine invertebrates. At one time, because of their slow speed and near-shore feeding habits, they were hunted nearly to extinction for their oil. However, over fifty years ago a moratorium was placed upon hunting them and, since that time, their numbers have increased dramatically.

Also ensuring their comeback is the fact that grey whales reproduce every second year, unlike some species of whale who give birth only every fifth year. The mating is an incredibly moving oceanic ballet, choreographed by a master hand. Two males swim alongside a female in heat and each nuzzles and stimulates her. Finally the female turns and accepts one male while the second cradles and steadies her body. After giving birth twelve months later, the female shares, with an older female, the nurturing of the baby whale thus increasing the chances of the survival of the species.

While not as dramatically beautiful or as streamlined as their cousins the orca (more commonly known as the killer whale), the grey whales of the Pacific have demonstrated surprising intelligence and a desire to communicate with humans. Shari determined to study them and, with a friend, purchased a used, 16-foot Zodiac, which enabled them to approach the whales at sea level. Acquaintances began to ask if they could accompany them and were willing to pay for the experience. From this humble beginning they eventually formed a whale watching charter business, one of the first on the west coast.

On a sunny day in April, 1985, Shari nosed out into the ocean off Lennard Light with her first boat-load of paying customers, in search of whales feeding in the wild. Suddenly, as if waiting for them, a grey blew close by and then proceeded to swim under the rubber boat. The thirty ton mammal slowly rose, gently cradling the small craft and its scarcely breathing humans for several minutes. It seemed an auspicious beginning for the fledgling business. Since then Shari has often experienced a whale sighting the Zodiac, eyeing it curiously, then altering course to swim toward it, as if making a conscious effort to communicate with the humans aboard.

Each year a few whales leave the migration to feed in the nourishing waters of Clayoquot Sound, rejoining the main body of whales in the fall for the southward trek. These friendly whales delight the local residents who celebrate their presence in music and art. The first time Shari encountered one of the "friendlies" the great grey, with its several-million-year-old smile, actually rested its massive head against the pontoon of the Zodiac and allowed itself to be petted and scratched. She said later, "It blew all my circuits."

Since time immemorial the waters of the northern Pacific have been home to a variety of whales. The humpback, right, sperm, and grey whales were only some of the species of these magnificent ocean mammals that enriched this corner of the planet by their great numbers. The story of their relentless slaughter by man has been one of unbridled greed and ignorance. The whales were hunted for their blubber which was rendered to oil, known as train. This rich marine oil was used for everything from fuelling lamps, cooking, and lubricating, to preserving food and softening leather. Ambergris, a substance found in the alimentary tract, was used in fine perfumes and spermaceti oil, drained from the head, was used in cosmetics and candles. Their baleen plates were utilized as stiffeners in shirt collars and women's corsets. Their ravaged corpses were left to rot on the beaches, the stench carrying for miles. Entire species were hunted to extinction in the belief that man had been given dominion over all the other species inhabiting the earth and its oceans. And so today Vancouver Island, once known as "the island of whales," has few resident species, and the twice-yearly migration of the great greys takes on special significance, becomes a cause for celebration.

How fitting that Clayoquot Sound, formerly a port of call for whaling ships on their way to the killing grounds, has become a centre for whale research and commercial whale watching. Modern day whale watching provides a unique educational opportunity, a chance to see these gentle behemoths of the sea in their natural habitat. Shari reasons that no one who has had the mystical experience of communing with the docile greys out on the cold grey waters of the Canadian Pacific will ever forget it. Nor will they remain unmoved when the environment of the marine mammals is threatened by various man-made catastrophes.

FOURTEEN

Renaissance Woman

During the sixties the west coast became a haven for some of the disenchanted youth of North America. They came from the cities and from the towns, they came with not much more than the clothes on their backs, and they came seeking answers to questions that had in the past been deemed irrelevant, perhaps unworthy. They built lean-tos on the beach and lived off the land to a large extent. Most eventually left, to return to life in the mainstream, and today the beaches lie white and undisturbed once again. Some, however, chose to stay, and their presence today, frequently in the forefront as winds of change sweep the area, is keenly felt. Within Clayoquot Sound lie innumerable islands of various shapes and sizes. Very often the only sign of habitation may be a wisp of smoke rising above the trees, a glimpse of a fishing boat anchored in a bay, or footsteps in the sand. These people are the new breed of west coaster, passionately in love with the area and totally committed to preserving its riches for generations to come.

I had been invited to a solstice party. Summer solstice, longest day of the year and occasion for celebration. Early that evening I met Susanne and her husband Steve at their boat which was tied up at the Government Dock in Tofino and made the acquaintance of their son Matt, twelve, and daughters Cosy, eight, and Misty, three years younger. We left the dock and moved out into the channel, making one stop along the way to pick up three passengers, then continued northward to Vargas Island. Vargas is the third largest island in the Sound and was named by Spanish explorers in the eighteenth century. Many years later, English immigrants attempted to settle the island but found its marshy soil entirely unsuited for farming and eventually abandoned their efforts. Today the island has largely returned to its natural state.

At the entrance to a small bay Steve cut the motor and we drifted toward large, barnacle-encrusted rocks. Several other boats were anchored nearby. Clambering over the side of the boat, we made our way, with varying degrees of agility, over the rocks and storm-tossed logs to the path that led past the small, family-run sawmill up to the house where our hosts stood in the doorway. Marilyn works alongside husband Neil on their tree farm and makes the daily crossing to Tofino perched astride the freshly cut lumber in their open herring skiff: in summer a lovely trip, in winter a test of endurance. Many an evening I've watched from the comfort of my lodging while Marilyn backs their large flat-bed truck down the Crab Dock, with scant inches to spare on either side, as effortlessly as I might park at a shopping mall. She then helps direct the unloading of the timber.

We were invited to fill our plates from a table that groaned under its load of smoked salmon and cod, fresh caught crab, clams and oysters, baskets of freshly baked bread and buns, cheeses, and potato salad in a colourful pottery bowl the size of a baby's bath. Friends gathered in small knots throughout the gracious home, discussing everything from the vagaries of oyster farming to the rally the following day on the grounds of the legislature building in Victoria in support of preserving the Carmanah Valley and its old growth stands of timber. Some joked that the gathering was also a going-away party for C.J. who was to begin serving his three-week jail sentence the following day, having been found guilty of civil disobedience during the Sulphur Passage stand-off the previous summer.

Later a fire was lit and many, including the children, danced. Summer solstice marks the beginning of the busiest season of the year for those who earn their livelihood from the sea and it might be months before these west coasters had an opportunity to visit again. I slipped away and went down to walk the beach, orienting myself by the lights of Kakawis and Opitsaht winking across the water. Close to midnight the party began to break up. Parents gathered up their sleepy children and we all began to make our way back to the boats.

We moved through the inky darkness of Father Charles Channel toward Wickaninnish Island, named for the Indian chief who ruled the Clayoquots. I turned to watch the magical stars-in-the-water phenomenon produced by luminous plankton, churned up by the boat's wash. We inched toward the shore where, by the rather feeble beams of our flashlights, our three passengers leapt nimbly onto the rocks and melted into the darkness. We continued around the point into a circular bay when I suddenly noticed the first quarter moon, like a slice of mandarin orange, rising to the east, and laying a ribbon of molten gold across the water, as if to guide us home. While Steve secured the boat, the rest of us scrambled over the side into the icy water, quickly waded ashore and made our way through the forest and up to the house, which is located on the outer side of the island. I fell asleep that night to the sound of the pounding surf beneath my pillow.

The next morning I rose early, eager to see by daylight what I had been able to catch only tantalizing glimpses of the night before. Seen from a distance, the house, constructed of local cedar and weathered by the years, appeared as one with the precipitous cliff that rose above a tiny cove below. It was framed, as if in quotation marks, by wind-sculptured pine trees. I followed the path behind the house which led to the leeward side of the island, back to the quiet bay where the boat lay anchored. I passed the chicken coop and Susanne's steep-roofed studio, then came upon Steve's boathouse where the skeleton of a fishing boat, half-clad in red cedar, stood on the blocks, already a thing of beauty. Down on the beach a bald eagle perched in a tree above the bay while a small mink scurried along the shore and hoof-prints in the sand testified to the presence of deer on the island.

Back at the house, after a hearty breakfast of brown egg omelettes and toast, Susanne prepared to leave for a day at the Sacred Circle Museum and Gallery, which she recently opened in Tofino. The gallery has become a showplace for local native art and artifacts. The name reflects the philosophy of those who believe that every living thing upon the earth is part of a sacred circle of interdependent creatures, whose ageless existence has been determined by forces ever beyond our understanding and control. Matt would take his mother over to the village in his Zodiac and stay for a day of surfing with friends. Once they left, Steve and I lingered over coffee savouring a philosophical discussion—backed by solid scientific evidence—on how fragile were our idyllic surroundings and how numerous the attacks upon them. In the background Cosy competently prepared a picnic lunch for us to take to the beach while Misty searched for her elusive blue beach sandals.

That afternoon, while Steve worked on the new addition to the house, the girls and I swam in the sheltered cove, beachcombed for driftwood and shared the delicious lunch. Among other things, I discovered the joy of eating marbled cheese, liberally spread with mayonnaise, washed down with cool spring water and consumed on a warm beach with friends. Cosy proudly showed me the secluded tree-shaded cul-de-sac on the sandy beach where she had been born. A very special place we all agreed, and recorded it for posterity by taking pictures. The girls explained to me that Misty was born at home while poor Matt entered the world in a hospital. He made his appearance prematurely while his parents were returning from a trip down east.

Later, as we sat munching apples, the girls told me about their pet fawn Buffy. Their father had found her in the woods and discovered that the mother had been slain by hunters, so brought the orphaned animal home. The little deer quickly adopted the family, following the children everywhere, even sleeping on top of their beds at night. "She was the best pet that anyone could ever have" Cosy said, "and we all loved her dearly." All went well until one day they discovered Buffy lying dead on the beach, "shot through the heart."

That evening, after a delicious supper of freshly caught salmon and organically grown vegetables from their cliffside garden, we sat talking over coffee. Susanne was born in Guelph, Ontario where her father was an agrologist and former member of parliament. Some of her fondest memories are of visits to her grandparents on their farm nearby, helping milk the cows and riding the tractor on her grandfather's knee. Her family later moved to Montreal and Susanne attended McGill University where she majored in languages and fine art. After graduation she took an additional three years training in graphic design at a French university. She was one of the artists chosen to create the "Man and His World" display after Expo '67.

In 1970 she moved west, spending the summer on the beach at Wreck Bay on Vancouver Island, making friends and relishing the heady freedom of that lifestyle. Back in Vancouver, while pounding the pavement looking for work (with little success), she ran into acquaintances from Long Beach who were heading south to surf California waters. Suddenly she knew that she couldn't return to a nine-to-five existence in the big city. Passing a small park, she threw her portfolio, high heels, and stockings behind a bush, unpinned her hair and walked barefoot through the streets of the city, determined to return to a freer lifestyle. From that moment on she never looked back.

Susanne rented space in Gastown, where she set up a design studio called "Metalmorphosis." She began to create and sell wall tapestries and large sensuous metallic mobiles full of colour and light that today hang in corporate buildings across Canada. She later opened a second shop dubbed "Ironmongers," that featured her antique metal jewellery. However, when her life seemed in danger of becoming regimented again, she sold every-thing, including her beloved motorcycle, and headed "by instinct" for the west coast of Vancouver Island. Once there, she rented a cabin on Long Beach and set up a small art studio which flour-ished until the government expropriated the land to become part of the new Pacific Rim National Park.

At this time Susanne met and fell in love with Steve, a tall handsome Ojibway Indian, born in Kenora, Ontario. Steve's family moved to Victoria where his mother died when he was only four. His father subsequently found it impossible to care for the child. During the next few years Steve grew up in a succession of government group homes and came to live for the summers spent at wilderness centres up-island. His life improved consider-ably when, at the age of twelve, he was adopted by a psychologist in Victoria. He eventually returned to the west coast of the island to live and work amongst the native people of the area. It was a time of re-discovering his roots and establishing his identity. Years later, his quest culminated in a visit to Kenora, accompanied by Susanne and the children, to visit his ancestral home and visit newly found relatives. Steve became a fisherman (herring and tuna) and master boat builder. Susanne and Steve have spent some of the happiest days of their lives living aboard their boat and fishing the waters of the Pacific coast, from Victoria to the Queen Charlotte Islands and southern Alaska.

When Susanne became pregnant with their first child they decided to look for a place to settle, and eventually bought property on historic Wickaninnish Island, a short distance from Tofino. It was here, in 1811, that the trading ship *Tonquin*—owned

Home – Wickaninnish Island

by John Jacob Astor, and registered in Boston—was blown up and sunk, with the loss of its crew, following a bitter disagreement between its captain and the Clayoquots.

The young couple decided to build their home on a promontory on the windward (sunset-side) of the island. By boat they beachcombed the shores of the various islands nearby for logs. They would then tow the logs to Neil and Marilyn's saw-mill on Vargas Island and for each two logs thus delivered, they would receive one back, cut into usable lengths. After clearing the site they began the formidable task of constructing the house. Steve would load the boat with lumber and bring it into the tiny cove directly beneath the cliff and then he and Susanne would painstakingly—by a means of pulleys and block and tackle—winch the boards up and over the precipice. The entire operation depended upon the tides and the temper of the ocean. It took twenty-five medium sized logs to build the house. Susanne kept healthy and agile throughout this time and the house indeed became a "labour of love."

Today the outside of the house has weathered to a silvery sheen. Out on the wrap-around deck there is a surprisingly small solar panel which generates enough power—both from sunlight and reflected light from the surface of the ocean—to run the family's radio-telephone, electric lights, and small television. Susanne has a propane-powered refrigerator, and a large wood stove which she uses for heating as well as cooking. She visits the laundromat in town to do her laundry. The main floor of the house consists of one large room—the ultimate "family room"—with indefinable boundaries delineating the kitchen, dining-room, office, living-room and guest bedroom. Upstairs is a large sleeping loft, reached by a ladder, which can be raised out of sight during the day. Doors and windows are usually open to the elements, permitting close harmony with the forces of nature that shape this family's lives.

The recent addition of a small, three-wheeled, all-terrain vehicle has made life easier for everyone, since all supplies must be landed in the bay on the leeward side and transported along the beach and through the forest to the house on the other side of the island. It has also proved valuable in hauling seaweed, culled from the surrounding waters for use as fertilizer in their beautiful cliffside garden.

What appears at first glance as a romantic way of living (and who has not fantasized about living on a picturesque island) is, in reality, a life that demands organization, flexibility, and a large ration of intestinal fortitude. However, for Susanne and Steve it is the only life they can envision, both for themselves and for their children.

The children love the island and, like young Robinson Crusoes, have explored much of it on foot. Susanne, with the aid of small computers, home-schools the children and finds their minds eager and questioning. She believes that children, if encouraged, are taught largely by living and doing, questioning and searching. The family travels widely throughout the Pacific Northwest on environmentally related matters, visiting native communities as well as white and, wherever they go, the children learn new skills, whether it be kayaking and spelunking or the ways of the forest. The great outdoors is their classroom and, perhaps because of this, the children are wonderfully wise.

During the years that Steve and Susanne fished the waters of the west coast they formed close links with the native people of the area and also became warm friends with Cougar Annie at Boat Basin, who became a great favourite with the children. In recent years, however, both have become increasingly concerned about the desecration of the rainforest, and the resulting depletion of natural resources. Finally, in 1979, after viewing first-hand the ravages of current forestry practices such as clearcut logging and slash-burning taking place on the west coast, they, together with other concerned citizens of the area, formed the nucleus of the "Friends of Clayoquot Sound." The family spent one turbulent winter living on Meares Island in support of native land claims. The whole Meares struggle was an intense emotional experience and one that proved to be the catalyst in forming an historic alliance between natives and environmentalists.

In 1982 the couple was commissioned by the Western Canada Wilderness Society to produce a film illustrating the effects of clearcut logging on the fishing industry of the west coast. They explored the coast by boat for several weeks, visiting remote areas where they filmed salmon spawning creeks choked by debris and denuded mountainsides which allowed the precious life-giving top soil to be washed into the sea, and recorded the absence of wild life. Entitled *British Columbia Chainsaw Massacre,* it is considered a classic by conservationists. Later the couple produced a film documenting the existence of archaeological ruins on the coast, one that proved vital in the legal struggle to support and establish native land claims. These experiences were such eye openers and the situations that they revealed so alarming, that both redoubled their efforts to educate the public to the dangers that exist when some resources are allowed to be exploited to the detriment of others.

And so, over the years, with their increasing involvement in environmental issues as they relate to the Pacific northwest and beyond, both Susanne and Steve have become knowledgeable, albeit controversial, "voices for the forest." Living in an area that for many years has based its economy on the harvesting of natural resources, their strong beliefs have made them pariahs among certain segments of the west coast population. This has not stopped them. Despite incidents of vandalism directed against them (boat set adrift, van trashed), they continue to protest clearcut logging and all its ramifications. During the Sulphur Passage standoff in 1988, both were leaders in the protest movement and both paid a stiff price.

Back on Wickaninnish Island the second morning of my visit dawned sunny and warm, and after breakfast I said my goodbyes to Steve and the children and accompanied Susanne down to the boat. As we crossed Templar Channel, she confided that she had just learned that once again she was expecting a child and the news, while welcome, was taking some getting used to. She also spoke of how the twice daily crossings, while taking considerable time and effort, had become much valued parentheses to her day. She explained, with some emotion, that, no matter how stressful a day had been or how discouraged she felt, the trips through these historic waters never failed to bring her a sense of renewal, a resurgence of energy, and an acute feeling of oneness with the elements of nature around her. It is at these times that she gathers her inner resources and strengthens her commitment to bettering our understanding of, and respect for, nature and its riches.

FIFTEEN

Clearcut Justice

The night air was split by hoarse cries and lights kept coming down the mountainside. "Don't come up any further—they are coming down after you," called the young man who was seated in a basket chair slung 60 feet above the ground in a tall spruce tree. For three days he had been resisting various threats and intimidations, including being shot with a pellet gun. His friends, who had been attempting to get to him, were afraid to turn on their flashlights, and crashed through the underbrush desperately trying to find cover. They had been trained not to run but violence was now directed against them and they felt they had no choice if they were to survive. "We'll break your legs," one of the loggers yelled, and directed his crew to spread out and search the surrounding woods.

Sulphur Passage, summer 1988, and terror ruled the night. What had, until that time, been a peaceful demonstration protesting the building of logging roads in the area, suddenly turned menacing when a crew of loggers arrived to cut down a tree that held a protester. By some miracle, perhaps a "gift of the forest," the tree, when felled, rather than falling over the cliff, got hung up in the trees next to it and Paul escaped unhurt. When the protesters were able to regroup, they radioed a distress call to the police who did not answer. Next, they requested help from the Coast Guard who replied that the situation, being on land, was out of their jurisdiction.

Unbeknownst to the loggers, Susanne and Julie had been filming the action from behind a tree further up the slope. Eventually they made their way back to their boat and returned to Tofino where friends Maureen and John made copies of the dramatic film. The original was given to the police to hold as evidence and one was sent out to the C.B.C. where it aired on national television that night. The two young women then returned to the beleaguered environmentalists at Sulphur Passage.

Once again the issue of clearcut logging versus sustainable development had fractionalized the residents of the west coast. An uneasy truce had prevailed in the area since the Meares Island moratorium had been declared three years previously. The first intimation of trouble came when one of the local politicians was quoted in the *Westerly News* as saying, "Logging is coming to this community and we have to be ready for it." The pronouncement had the chilling sound of a *fait accomplit*. Some citizens of the village began to clear their land to build rental accommodation and parking lots for the crew vehicles. Still others in the community paused, and drew deep within themselves for the strength that would be needed in the days to come as they once again prepared to stand united against a powerful multi-national company.

First, the concerned citizens asked the company to present their plans for logging in the area to the Tofino village council. This they refused to do. At this time, knowing full well what the consequences of their action could be, the Friends of Clayoquot Sound, backed by the Chamber of Commerce, sent a carefully worded telegram to the provincial government:

*The Friends of Clayoquot Sound are planning immediate
action to halt the road construction presently near the Sulphur
Pass area of Shelter Inlet in Clayoquot Sound. We request a
moratorium on the clearcut logging of old growth forest in
Clayoquot Sound pending a full plan on sustainable development for the area. Await immediate reply.*

The reply never came.

Eventually, a meeting was arranged between executives
of the logging company and members of the Friends (including
native people) whose livelihood would be directly threatened by
clearcut logging in the Sound. The meeting took place in the village school and the executives were rather disconcerted to find
themselves seated in a circle, interspersed among the Friends,
rather than holding court from behind their customary desks.
From the beginning it appeared obvious that the two groups
would find it nearly impossible to find any common ground.
Finally the native leader left, completely disheartened, and after
that the meeting limped to its conclusion. The officials stated that
the company remained determined to construct a road in Sulphur
Passage for the purpose of clearcut logging. This, in one of Clayoquot Sound's last remaining untouched inlets. As soon as this pronouncement was made, sixty people rose as one and said, "See you
in the morning."

At dawn the next day there were ten small boats headed
for Shelter Inlet, carrying forty young men and women who had
left families, oyster farms, fishing grounds, and small shops to man
a blockade of the road for as long as it would take to bring some
resolution to the situation. They were a ragged little band of volunteers, but they had the dedicated zeal of freedom fighters.
Throughout history just such groups have often turned the tide in
the affairs of man. For the next four months they would place
themselves in the blast zone, adhering, with no small amount of
valour, to the principles of passive resistance in the face of threats
and intimidation.

Spirit of Clayoquot Sound

Some pitched tents or slept under tarpaulins while others preferred to sleep on beds made from boughs or on rough platforms constructed amid the branches of the large trees. There was a hastily organized system of ferrying supplies from the village of Tofino to the camp. There was always a guitar among the group and in the evenings they sat around a small campfire and sang. When the rains came, as they often did, the area turned muddy and it could be days before they had dry clothes or warm food. They drew great comfort from each others presence, in an atmosphere that daily became increasingly hostile.

And so the long, turbulent weeks passed. One day two young women took defensive positions in front of a stand of tall spruce trees about to be felled to make way for the road. The foreman called in the Sherman tank that was used for blasting and the drill was lowered across their shoulders to the rock wall behind. The situation was at a stalemate and the police were called. When they arrived, they removed the women, saying, "No one stops the logging industry in British Columbia." The blasting continued. Another time, after Susanne had received permission to camp on the nearby Indian reserve, a process server woke her at 5:00 A.M. and when she emerged from the tent into the pouring rain, he snapped her picture and said, "What's the matter Susanne, don't you like wake-up call?"

The situation continued until finally the logging company decided to lay charges. The police culled eleven people from amongst the forest protectors, including Steve, Susanne, Shari and four other young women. They were placed in handcuffs and flown to Vancouver where they appeared before a judge who bound them all over for trial in the district court in Nanaimo several weeks hence. They were then released, with a restriction that forbade them to appear, for any reason, within a three mile radius of Sulphur Pass. Others stepped forward and took their places in the forest.

Eventually thirty-five conservationists were arrested that summer and charges were laid against twenty-eight of them. The first group appeared in September when, upon the advice of their lawyers, they pleaded guilty to civil contempt of court. They each received fines of up to one thousand dollars and were ordered to apologize to the court.

The second group, appearing in court in November, chose to defend themselves. They mounted a spirited but reasoned defense of their beliefs and their actions, one that earned the judge's grudging respect. However, at the end of the week-long trial the verdict went against them. Depending upon their degree of involvement, each person was required to pay a fine, (up to $1,000.00) serve time in jail (which varied from five days to six weeks), or both. In giving his reasons for the judgement, the honourable justice had this to say:

> ...*Before I end this judgement I must recognize the honest sincerity of all the defendants. Their cause is a noble one. They look upon themselves as a small bank of protectors of this beautiful area of British Columbia which God has bestowed upon us. They see any manmade intrusion upon it as an exterminating force which will eventually cause everlasting devastation. They believe society is wrong in permitting it to happen. They may be right. However, a court of law cannot decide these issues. The matter is political in nature... It seems absolutely clear the issues which the law calls upon me to decide in these proceedings are not the issues which the defendants hoped to decide by coming here this week. I regret this to be so, but that is the way our system functions... As sympathetic as I may be to their concerns, I have sworn duty to uphold the law, notwithstanding my own private thoughts. Although political action is fraught with difficulty and requires hard, concentrated, and organized work, it is the only method we have yet discovered until someone finds a better way.*

At the end of that long, bitter summer, the logging company halted road construction at Sulphur Pass.

The conservationists, having been given six months to either pay their fines or serve their jail sentences, returned to their homes on the west coast. In the weeks that followed, they sat together and discussed the issues, weighing the consequences of either course of action. They all felt strongly against paying money into a system which they felt allowed the destruction of the environment. They also hoped that perhaps the surrounding publicity of their actions would serve to illustrate the depth of their commitment and heighten public awareness of the issues at stake. In the end they decided, without exception, to surrender themselves to the authorities for incarceration in one of Her Majesty's penal institutions.

So it was, on the morning of April 26th. 1989, a small caravan of vehicles left Tofino at first light to make the five-hour trip to Victoria. By 10:00 A.M. the group was gathered together in front of the courthouse, being interviewed by the media. Soon thereafter, the men in the group were escorted to the Nanaimo Correctional Centre. While time dragged on, Shari stood to one side chatting with friends. She was three months pregnant and clutched a bottle of vitamins given to her by a well-wisher with which she planned to supplement her diet in the coming days. Steve and the children were there for Susanne. This type of situation was not entirely new to the family as Steve had more than once served time in jail on similar charges, but it would be the first time the children had ever been separated from their mother. Susanne and Steve had spent a sleepless night wrestling with the tempting option of simply paying the hefty fine so that Susanne could remain at home with the children. Toward morning she made her decision and finally slept. She explained her choice to the children over breakfast and all three calmly accepted the news. Matt told her that he understood why she had to leave the family and that he was proud of her.

The six women had been told by their lawyers to expect to be sent to half-way homes somewhere on the island. Instead, they were unceremoniously bundled into a paddy wagon and found themselves headed for the airport. It was later revealed that,

at the last minute, word had come down that if they were determined to do time, they would be required to do hard time. Finally
they were told that they would be incarcerated at Oakalla, maxi-
mum security prison outside Vancouver. When they heard those
words, chills ran down their spines.

Upon arrival at the penitentiary, they were kept waiting
in the small admitting room for several hours. The authorities there
had not been notified of their imminent arrival and were forced to
make hasty arrangements. By this time Shari was feeling faint and
the other women stood so that she could lie down. Finally, they
were told to shower and wash their hair with disinfectant. All personal effects were taken away, including Shari's vitamins and herb
tea and Susanne's art supplies. They were placed in the segregation
unit with, among others, two women (Frenchie and Tinkerbelle)
serving time for murder. Both were very intimidating to the newcomers and among other things, smoked constantly in the
confined area. Also in the unit was an anti-abortionist who had
received threats against her life by the two women.

Back in Victoria, Steve and the children were staying
with Peg, longtime friend and mentor from Long Beach. When
he found out where his wife and the other women had been
taken, he began lobbying on their behalf. He spent hours on the
phone, talking with government officials and lawyers and eventually his efforts succeeded in having the women moved to another
building within the prison grounds called the Doukhobour
House. This was a more open setting and life became more routine. To their delight they discovered a beautiful ring-necked
pheasant who spent his days on the grounds outside their windows
and promptly named him Jonathan Livingston Pheasant. They
saved tidbits of food for him, and envied him his freedom. Each
morning they were awakened at 7:30 A.M., to a breakfast of por-
ridge and weak coffee. The meals were standard prison fare: no
juice or fresh fruit was available, even vegetables were a rarity. In
the time honoured tradition of passive disobedience, Susanne

chose to fast during her entire time in confinement, taking only fluids. Everyone was assigned various housekeeping chores such as waxing and polishing floors. While conditions had improved, each young west coast woman yearned for the outdoors and eventually they were allowed outside for a brief time each afternoon.

During this time each woman drew immeasurable strength from the presence of her friends and together they composed a letter to the newspapers:

We are the six women of Tofino serving time for protecting our old growth rainforests. While we were being tried for blockading Fletcher Challenge's attempts to build a logging road into Sulphur Passage, one of the island's last entirely unlogged inlets, an interesting thing was happening. The same company was being fined $50,000.00 for wood wastage in Clayoquot Sound. A few months later the company admitted to overcutting as the reason for the layoffs of 450 employees in the Victoria area. In view of this and out of love for our area, we remain committed to exposing bad logging practices. While we spend time in jail, the real criminals, the forest companies, continue to exploit the forests and degrade the fragile soil. As people inform themselves of the forest atrocities in British Columbia there will be more and more of us willing to spend "time" to stop the destruction. We have little time left. No more clearcuts!...

After five days most of the women were released. They had been told that they would be provided with bus tickets home. However, when the time came, they were told it wasn't possible. For Shari it was the last straw and "something snapped." She told the policewoman "The penal system shipped us over here and it is up to them to ship us back." The woman replied that she didn't have the authority to write the tickets and since it was Sunday she didn't wish to disturb her superior. The other women, anxious to be on their way entreated Shari not to belabour the point but Shari was adamant. It was the principle of the thing she explained and she wasn't leaving before she had her bus ticket!

Finally, in desperation, the guard phoned her supervisor, got permission to write the tickets and the tree huggers were on their way. A woman reporter from the Vancouver Sun picked them up outside and they all went to Granville Island for breakfast.

Left behind in prison were Susanne and Julie, who had both been sentenced to an extra three days for their part in making the film and ensuring that it was broadcast on national television. On the morning they were released, Steve and the children were waiting outside the prison walls and it was a happy, if somewhat shaken group that drove into Tofino later that day. Several days later, as Susanne prepared to open the gallery, a note was delivered to her. It was addressed to all the forest protectors who went to jail for their beliefs, and read, "Thank you for going to jail for the rest of us. You were in our thoughts and prayers." It was signed by a young woman who worked in the village office.

The memories of those frightening, dehumanizing days in prison will never leave any of the people who served time, many still suffer from nightmares. And yet, with delicious irony, many have come to feel that the experience actually empowered them. Today Shari says, "We paid the highest price possible and, scary as it was, it only served to strengthen my commitment." Susanne adds, "We do not enter these situations lightly. We know what the consequences of our actions may be and we are willing to pay the price in order to save these last stands of temperate rainforest. Whatever the next step is, we are ready for it. Our commitment is absolute."

SIXTEEN

The Inlet

Comes the morning I wake,
and gaze onto the ever changing panorama of the inlet.
On sunny days each detail three dimensional,
washed in fragile natural light.
Surrounded by mountains,
each tree standing alone.
Lone Cone, Meares Island, oft wreathed in cloud.
Small islands, each steeped in history.
One, Dead Man's Isle,
where years ago natives laid their dead in tree tops.
Another, Tibb's Island,
where a lonely Englishman erected a castle and
called the spot Dream Isle.

Snug harbour, wherein fishing boats
bob at the quay.
At night tiny village all

unto itself.
Lights wink, pungent aromas mingle
with salt air.

Quiet voices discuss the day's labour,
jobs well done.
Drama understated, shrugged off
with laugh or curse.
By early morning silver light,
the fishing fleet has gone.

At low tide outcroppings of rock appear,
quickly covered by sleek black cormorants.
Seen from a distance they resemble
a coven of witches.
The passing of seaplanes cause most
to take flight,
in long, black, undulating line.
Raucous gulls, and crows, and
saucy little kingfishers.
Ducks, and mergansers, and
wheeling flocks of tiny little shorebirds.
All giving sound and motion to the scene.

The inlet has a matriarch, so dignified and wise.
At low tide she and her mate stand
feeding mid-thigh in water.
The Great Blue Heron
is the unquestioned ruler here.
When she flies in, after feeding up the inlet,
the shallows belong to her.

I thought it an optical illusion
the first time I saw her

walk on water,
in the middle of the inlet.

On second glance, I realized the tide was receding,
she was standing on a mud flat,
scant inches below the surface.
With a fluff of one wing, she encouraged the male
to find his own grazing spot.

Often in the early evening she'll swoop down,
landing awkwardly on the dock.
The small boats are in,
lined up as if for inspection.
With queenly stride she moves along the planks.
Occasionally stopping, craning long neck
into a boat to snatch a tidbit
the fisherman has neglected.

Some days I rise to sheer curtains of rain
being pulled across the inlet.
The colours now are monotone—
a subtler shade of scene.
All mountains ringed in cloud.
The pulse goes on as ever, the ebb and flow of tide.
Wheeling hawk and heron, oblivious to the change.

Sometimes I am drawn, reluctantly,
to the city.
I encumber myself with schedules,
people to meet, places to go.
At last I am driving back along lake and river,
forest rising on each side.
The air is rushing in at me, saltier with each turn.
Then I know.

My heart tells me I'm coming home,
first glimpse of the inlet reaffirms it.
My heart and soul reside here now—
I know they always will.

Epilogue

I didn't start out to write a book with an environmental perspective but it would be lessening the experience, weakening my covenant with the people of the west coast were I to allow the reader to assume that the region is an untroubled paradise. Beneath the idyllic vistas of crashing surf, gentle tree-clad mountains and sparkling inlets lie immense problems, problems that threaten to tear the fabric of west coast life beyond repair.

When I first began this project I felt it was unfair that the sparsely inhabited coast should be forced to bear the brunt of these grave environmental problems. However, as time went on and I began to know the area and its people, I came to see the west coast as a microcosm of the world and to believe that if these far-reaching problems could be solved, these were the people who would do it. Perhaps their presence on the Canadian coast at this time in the earth's evolution is no accident.

The concept of sustainable development continues to struggle as the voices for studied use of the region's valuable natural resources repeatedly clash with those who would reap their bonanza today. The problems are vastly more complex than the simplistic equation of scenery-versus-jobs as some are anxious to have us believe. As long as the solutions to even the most basic problems are seen as mutually exclusive, very little progress will be made. As long as people are not listening to each other and caring about other's needs and aspirations, very little will be accomplished.

While committees are formed and studies are funded, seminars held and tours carefully arranged, the relentless ravage of Canadian rainforests continues unabated. Decisions are made in boardrooms in Japan or New Zealand which eventually alter the lives and livelihoods of people in Canada, most particularly the west coast. Communities are increasingly feeling isolated from, and helpless to influence or have any input into, the decision making process. Perhaps the time has come (some would say belatedly) for communities to take control of their own resources and to work toward accommodating the different aspects of the region's dynamics.

As long as we allow ourselves to be pressured into believing that one livelihood, be it oyster farming, whale watching, or logging, takes precedence over another, we will continue to be in conflict with one another. As long as short term thinking governs our actions, our hopes for the future will be defeated.

We must keep faith with the generations who have gone before us, most of whom never could have imagined the complexities of the problems we face today. More importantly, we must prepare for the generations that will follow us. The time has come to return to the precepts of stewardship, to the concept that recognizes "we are only passing through."

The treasures of our forests are not fully understood yet, nor their numbers inventoried. Ancient peoples believed the giant trees held the secrets of the universe, and, with recent discoveries of drugs which hold great promise for mankind being extracted from their bark, the age-old faith seems to be increasingly borne out. We must recognize the blessed truth that, as human beings, we are but a small component of the natural world, and must learn to live in rhythm with and show respect for that which surrounds us. Who can possibly believe, in their deepest of beings, that we are all knowing, and were set upon this earth to subdue and conquer, whether our subjects be the whales of the deep or the giants of the living forest?

Future generations will surely question why, in the closing years of the twentieth century, a supposedly enlightened nation such as Canada, continued to allow—in the face of well documented evidence as to the environmental perils it invited—the sale, to the highest bidder, of one of its most precious natural resources, the temperate rainforest.

There are viable, profit-producing forest plantations, and there are clean bodies of water, they do exist. The challenge is to make them exist for everyone. In the final analysis, in the words of Greenpeace, *"We all live downstream."*

Printed on Recycled Paper
with Vegetable Based Inks

PRINTED IN CANADA BY MANNING PRESS